Wha

BREAK OUT

"BREAK OUT will help break down the stereotypes and bring down the barriers."

Tony Coelho
Author, AMERICANS WITH DISABILITIES ACT
former Congressman (D-California)

"Reads like a beautiful literary bouquet: full of color, thorns, and lasting fragrance."

Carol Roder, Marketing Manager
COLEMAN SPAS
Chandler, Arizona

"Analogous, metaphorical, humorous, and true . . . a medley of stories that presents a balanced perspective of life."

Urban Miyares, President
DISABLED BUSINESSPERSONS ASSOCIATION
San Diego, California

" . . . Fractures assumptions with wisdom, determination."

Joan Behr, Vice President-Communication
FOREMOST FARMS USA
Baraboo, Wisconsin

" . . . This talented man confronts the stereotyped images of those physically impaired."

Dr. Harley A. Swiggum
Founder of the ADULT CHRISTIAN EDUCATION FOUNDATION and Author of the BETHEL SERIES

BREAK OUT

Finding Freedom When You Don't Quite Fit The Mold

James R. Hasse, ABC

A Quixote Publication

ISBN 0-9633083-7-8

Quixote Publications
209 Best Street
Berea, Ohio 44017-2639

Library of Congress Cataloging-in-Publication Data

Hasse, James R., 1943-
Break out : finding freedom when you don't quite fit the mold/ James R. Hasse.
p. cm.
ISBN 0-9633083-7-8X (alk. paper)
1. Hasse, James R., 1943---Health. 2. Cerebral palsied--Wisconsin--Baraboo--Biography. 3. Executives--Wisconsin--Baraboo--Biography. 4. Handicapped--United States. I. Title.
RC388.H388 1996
362. 1' 96836' 0092--dc20
[B] 96-7718
CIP

These 51 true stories reflect the actual experiences of the author. However, names, locations, and descriptions of the main characters (other than immediate family members) and of some organizations have been changed to protect the privacy of the people involved.

To Mom and Dad, who through more questions than answers, provided the underpinnings I needed for a life of discovery and independence.

A Special Thank You

To my wife, Pam—fellow seeker and valued critic—for her inspiration and discernment.

To Lynn Nashban, my career counselor, for her challenge and encouragement.

To Patricia Mote, my editor and publisher, for her insight and guidance.

To Shirley Haugen, my associate, for editing each of these personal-experience stories.

To Helen Ziech, fellow church member, for her perspective.

To Helen Zuhlke and Sandy Grisham for their title suggestions.

To family, friends, associates, and strangers who have helped me to deal with reality.

Contents

Foreword

Jim Hasse personifies that element in the human spirit that seeks and finds shades of light in difficult circumstances.

Deeply introspective, he has found within himself a reservoir of courage that consistently prompts him to make adversity his friend.

Using his experiences as a person who has had cerebral palsy since birth, Hasse paints a portrait of his spirit in this series of short stories. That portrait reveals a predictable mixture of mood swings and emotions as this talented man confronts the stereotyped images of those physically impaired.

Yet the themes that shine through these poignant short stories are always upbeat, always encouraging, and always demonstrative of that something in all of us which can take any impairment, whatever its nature and whatever its source, and turn it into triumph.

The latter statement goes to the heart of what this book is about.

Dr. Harley A. Swiggum

Founder of the Adult Christian Education Foundation and Author of the Bethel Series

Preface

Draw your chair up close to the edge of the precipice,
and I'll tell you a story.
—F. Scott Fitzgerald
Notebooks

In a divided world and country, extremist views, quick answers, and homogenized insights often get the press coverage and broadcast time. "Maybe" and "I don't know yet" take too much time and are too tentative. They garner little credibility in much of the media.

Yet, on a personal level, most of us live with a larger reality. A part of our journey through life is settling for temporary "maybe" answers about who we can become. That's especially true when we need to face fundamental questions about how we can deal effectively with false assumptions about ourselves—and the presumptions others may form about us—because we don't quite fit accepted norms.

BREAK OUT offers you the opportunity to stretch that "maybe" side of your life. It will help you to discover something new about yourself and others, one story at a time.

Based on my collection of temporary predicaments, BREAK OUT is a series of "bedtime stories" for feeding your soul with some not-so-easy questions to think about the next morning. The questions may be universal, but the answers are unique to your particular temperament and circumstances.

Cookie-cutter solutions—unlike tested recipes from your favorite cookbook or step-by-step directions in your computer software manual—often provide little insight into some of life's stickiest problems.

BREAK OUT'S 51 short stories show there are no easy answers—only questions that, if answered honestly, can help you tussle effectively with reality if you're presumed different.

For many people, life is a continual, unconscious effort to narrow the gap between their own perceptions about who they are and the assumptions others make about them based on their appearance, gender, color, age, weight, height, abilities, temperament, and culture.

Narrowing that gap is not only society's challenge but an individual's responsibility. That process takes time, but it's worth the effort. Narrowing that gap is the foundation for achieving personal maturity.

JAMES R. HASSE, ABC
February 26, 1996

Chapter 1

Gaining Self-Assurance

Random Reprisal, Rigid Ritual

Patience, that blending of moral courage with physical timidity.

—Thomas Hardy
Tess of the D'Urbervilles

The other night I had a nightmare about patrolling the jungles of Vietnam.

No. I'm not a Vietnam vet. I haven't watched a Vietnam War movie since *Platoon,* and that was at least three years ago. And my memories of the nightly TV coverage of the war in Vietnam twenty years ago have long faded.

Still, I found myself struck by the deep fear of knowing our enemies, full of revenge, were silently watching us (even though we couldn't see them), as we marched fan-like across a field flanked by thick jungle.

The fear of imminent death stiffened my legs so I could hardly walk. Yet, I was on the move, forcing first one leg and then the other in front of me through the grass. I knew I could fall with the very next step by tripping a land mine or triggering sniper fire from the flanks.

I didn't realize what this was all about until I had a chance to think about it that morning. Then I knew.

I had walked down that same field of thick grass many times before. In some small way, maybe I have also known a tinge of what it's like to fear the random reprisals amid the rigid ritual of a military operation.

But it was not in the jungle. It was in church.

Sundays were traumatic for me when I was about ten. I dreaded going to our country church—a very formal, fundamentalist congregation that insisted on ushering people in and out of church, even though an attendance of sixty nearly filled the sanctuary.

At that time, I didn't walk with crutches. While I was relaxed and lifted by a feeling of inner confidence, I could walk unaided and override my lack of balance.

Yet, when self-consciousness gripped me, my leg muscles would tighten. I felt as if I were walking with two artificial legs—with little control, little balance—and I would stumble and fall into a heap.

Sunday mornings I would find myself struggling to keep up with our family when the usher would sweep down the center aisle of the church in front of us as if he were leading a parade.

Left behind—even though the distance between the front and back of the church was no longer than sixty feet—I would go through all kinds of contortions, trying to get my stiff legs moving forward and my wooden feet tracking in the right direction. The goal was to get down the aisle without falling.

Falling was no big deal when I was alone. Besides, I knew how to fall—how to, above all, protect my head. But that skill didn't come without some pain. I had numerous scars on the back of my head to mark the times I didn't protect it.

These *war wounds*—and the blood that flowed from them—gave me a healthy respect for falling. It was part of the natural order of things within my world.

But falling in public would be embarrassing because it would draw further attention to my condition and provide members of the congregation with another excuse for pity.

My walks down the church aisle were, I was sure, a sight to behold. I could feel people on both sides watching me, but I didn't dare look at the hurt in their eyes.

I didn't realize it then, but I now know I make some people uncomfortable. They are uncomfortable because my presence forces them to cope, in varying degrees, with their own insecurities about being physically vulnerable.

Perhaps that was the tension among the members of the congregation I felt as the ushers allowed the people in each pew to walk single file down the center aisle after each Sunday service was over. And I, again, would have to deal with my own insecurity—and try to reach the back of the church without falling.

Maybe that's part of the reason I experienced such a wide range of reactions from the members of the congregation (from unabashedly cold to stoically friendly) during those reserved visits outside the sanctuary after each Sunday morning service.

Were they dreading the day when I would fall going up or down the aisle, break the congregation's pompous formality, and force the members to react to me as a person?

Each Sunday I could feel the anticipation, and my palms would become sweaty and cold.

On Getting It Right

I have tried so hard to do the right.

—Grover Cleveland, last words

There were spent flash bulbs and empty film cases bulging out of my pockets as I continued to click away, taking picture after picture of grocery shoppers picking up Home Dairy milk from the supermarket's dairy case.

Joe, vice president of manufacturing, stood in one of the side aisles with the store's manager, watching as I switched film again. I needed both black-and-white prints as well as color transparencies, and I only had one camera.

Time was short. I knew it was 6:00 P.M. We were in Valparaiso, Indiana, and Joe and I had to get back to Wisconsin so we could be in the office the next morning.

Patience. I was always impressed by how patient he was with me—helping haul my clumsy camera and tripod into and out of cars and into dairy plants and even supermarkets.

I clicked off five more shots. I glanced at Joe and could see it was time to go.

"That's it," I finally said. "I'm all done."

"You sure you don't want any more?" Joe chided, chuckling with the store's manager.

It was my one opportunity to highlight Home Dairy milk, one of our consumer brands, in a major supermarket setting, and I didn't want to pass it up without getting some useable photography for our publications and our audio/visual programs.

Joe helped me load the camera equipment into the car and we took off for Wisconsin.

"Got a little carried away there," Joe said.

"Yeah," I replied weakly. "Good photography, though, is ninety percent luck. I have to take ten frames to get one good one."

"Depends on what you consider good," Joe teased.

"You have to bracket and all that—so you can get various exposures."

"All I know is that you blew your photography budget again on this trip," Joe kidded. "You're going to have twenty pictures of the same thing."

"The trick is to wait out your subject so they get used to you," I explained, more seriously, trying to justify the extra time we were spending at the supermarket. "That's when you get the good candid stuff—when people forget you're there, clicking away."

But Joe wasn't interested in my philosophy about taking good pictures.

"Fantastic dairy case, though," I offered.

"Right," Joe agreed. "One of our best customers."

He didn't understand why getting it right was important to me. At the time I didn't fully comprehend it either. I knew that I enjoyed my job as communication director because it gave me the opportunity to plot my progress in continually improving my work.

After all, in publication work, I could always shoot for a better product with the next issue. I started every month with a clean slate—a new issue to get out and new photos to take.

Yes, perseverance did yield improvement. But in the process, I made a lot of mistakes—photos that turned out blurry, feature stories that did not jell, business proposals that did not fly.

Failure, though, was a part of life. It was a lesson I had learned early. Walking straight, talking clearly, writing plainly—all required trial and error. There was always that one chance in ninety that I would someday get it right.

But, at thirty-two, I was as good, physically, as I was going to get. Intellectually, I accepted that, but as a first-child perfectionist, I inadvertently transferred my thirst for continual improvement to my work.

I'd try, try, and try again, despite the risk of becoming excessive in my pursuit of perfection.

And during the go-go business years of the 1980s, that made some portions of my life redundant to those who knew me best—associates, family, friends. I justified my try-again approach to corporate life by insisting that basic change in business is a long-term effort.

But the rewards were not going to those who worked to "get it right." They went to those who risked even more to move on to new cities, new firms, new people, and new challenges.

Joe had been right. I ended up with twenty very useable photos of people picking up Home Dairy milk from a dairy case. The persistence that served me well in my personal life was not always useful in the business world.

Moscow Fantasies

You feel mighty free and easy and comfortable on a raft.

— Mark Twain
Adventures of Huckleberry Finn

Her hair, dishwater blond, was long and straight. Every time she stood up to speak into the bus's public address system, it would tumble down the back of her stocky torso and plain, white cotton dress.

She wore no makeup and no stockings. She could have been a protester-for-peace student at Berkeley. Except she had stuffed her feet into white, stubby high heels—a capitalist fetish you'd never see on an American campus in 1970. And she carried a worn paperback copy of Mark Twain's *Adventures of Huckleberry Finn* with her almost everywhere we went.

I had just spent three days with Yvetna, our tour guide in Moscow. She would always give me the front seat behind the driver so I could avoid navigating the bus's narrow aisle and, instead, slide my crutches beneath the first seat.

The driver struggled to downshift manually as we jerked into the main entrance of the airport. The smell of gasoline came through the driver's window with the hot July breeze.

Yvetna stood in the aisle beside me and in slow but perfectly pronounced English spoke through the squeaky microphone. "We're now at the airport. Your flight leaves at 10:45—in one hour. Please have your passports ready as you go through the gate."

The gate. I dreaded the gate where we would individually pass through a series of cages, each separated by steel girders, so the military men could review our important documents. Stern-looking, clean-shaven men, armed with rifles, they appeared as hard as the bars they worked behind.

"We at Intourist thank you for visiting Moscow and wish you a safe journey home," Yvetna continued. "I've enjoyed meeting each of you."

Our group, twenty-five middle-aged people involved in Wisconsin agri-business, applauded, and she smiled. It was what I expected from a People-to-People delegation.

"Ready to go home?" Yvetna asked me, after she settled back into her seat.

I quietly said, "Yes."

Afer a week's tour of Moscow, St. Petersburg, and the Ukraine, I was tired. And I was worn by the continual strain of believing our group was being closely watched by the silent, stoic "fellow traveler" with the black briefcase who had suddenly joined our group with no introduction on the first day. We had visited a safe, stable country with vast resources. But it was also oppressive.

Perhaps I was depressed because the stalled elevators, poor customer service, and crumbling apartment buildings told me the Soviet system, by Western standards, was not working.

The tenets of a collective society were outlined in fliers formatted like the religious tracts we'd find stuck in our front doorsill back home. The Soviet fliers, stuffed in my airplane seat pocket and arranged neatly on my hotel room's desk, appealed to my idealism as a twenty-seven-year-old. But now I had tasted reality in the Soviet Union—the banality that came with the empty promises of achieving peace, providing jobs, and eliminating hunger.

Was my reality also evident to the Soviets? Marx's slogan, "From each according to his abilities, to each according to his *needs*," had been altered in the current literature found in my hotel room to read, "From each according to his abilities, to each according to his *work*."

The deception both amused and irritated me. I was disappointed to find both superpowers resorting to deceit because they underestimated the intelligence and fortitude of human beings. With a bastardized form of communism, the Soviets were seeking to duplicate the security and collective achievement Russians had gained under the czars. Caught in a Southeast Asian war that could not be won, the U.S. government was putting the CIA on college campuses to diffuse anti-war efforts in a society which valued individual freedom, choice, and success.

"We go to Copenhagen first," I finally replied more fully to Yvetna's query. Denmark. It would be the perfect escape from the stale communist overlay that shrouded the vibrant patchwork of cultures the Soviets had artificially gathered under one flag. "Then home."

I was always surprised. Yvetna understood me, despite my garbled speech, which often minced English into a series of undistinguishable vowels.

Because we were each aware of the double barrier between us, we may have listened to each other more intently, tried to understand more thoroughly, and appreciated more fully the communication, though superficial at times, that did occur.

An American tourist with cerebral palsy and Canadian crutches in Moscow was probably as unique in Yvetna's eyes as it was for me to watch her absorb *Huckleberry Finn*.

Did she realize how controversial *Huck Finn* had been when it was first published in the United States? Was she reading it to discover our fundamental weaknesses—the racial problems that permeate the fabric of our society? Did she understand us better than we understood ourselves?

I had watched her eyes during our three-day tour, trying to detect a hint of insincerity or a subtle glimmer that would indicate she did not wholeheartedly believe the party line. But I saw none.

Under questioning from our group, she skirted the issue about whether the Soviet government had closed churches in its ban against religion. The Soviet constitution guaranteed religious freedom, she said.

I tested her willingness to admit that many of Moscow's onion-shaped buildings, originally cathedrals, were designed by Italian architects. She did not know but said she would check and get back to me with an answer. The next day she weakly replied that my "assumption could not be verified."

And on the streets of Moscow, at the school we visited, and in the subway, I didn't see another person with a disability. It's more efficient, after all, in a collective society to warehouse people who are different. Odd-shaped widgets clog the machine.

Still, who could read *Huck Finn* and not feel the freedom of the Mississippi River?

As our bus stopped at the terminal, Yvetna hopped out and formally said goodbye to each person who descended the awkward steps of the bus.

Out of courtesy to the group, I waited until last. I was about to shake her hand, but then she hugged me, and I found my arms, still cuffed by my crutches, around her shoulders. She kissed me on my cheek.

Yvetna and I needed a river—and a raft.

Tangled Motivations

The mind is always the dupe of the heart.

—Francois Duc De La Rochefoucauld
Reflections

It was mid-October, and she was forcing herself to eat. By Thanksgiving she would go into the hospital for the last time. By Christmas she would be dead.

In the back of our minds, we all knew that could be how 1980 would end for our family. Our mother was slowly starving from stomach cancer, but we were not looking ahead three months. We were taking the inevitable steps one day at a time.

That's why inviting Kathy out to the farm for the first time to meet my family was so inappropriate. It complicated Mom's Saturday. Yet, from my sheltered workday life, it seemed right. After all, Kathy and I were good friends who worked in the same office.

Beyond that, we oddly complemented each other on several levels. Kathy had grown up in Whitefish Bay, a fashionable suburb of Milwaukee, and felt out of place in rural Wisconsin. I grew up on a farm in rural south central Wisconsin but longed for city life.

I had worked my way up to first-tier management and was just beginning to realize how our company's corporate culture worked. Kathy, a new college graduate in agricultural journalism, was dealing with the frustrations of her first job.

At twenty-three, Kathy feared she would end up someday like her mother, fighting chronic bouts with mental illness. At thirty-seven, I was discovering the loss a dying mother can feel in not being able to see her children accomplish all that they were about to achieve.

"Don't be afraid to go into a nursing home when the time comes that you can't take care of yourself," my mother would admonish me during my growing-up years. I would watch her hazel eyes go blank as she tried to anticipate how I would fare as a single, older adult.

Over the long months of treatment for her cancer, Mom continued to talk about the broad scope of life. I was trying to live in 1980—still trying to understand the psychological ramifications of living with my physical disabilities.

I was surprised Kathy had agreed to come to the farm. But we knew it was going to be one of the last nice weekends of the fall. And we knew it was probably going to be one of Mom's last weekends at home.

"This is Kathy," I said to Mom, as Kathy and I entered the old farmhouse. The kitchen table was set for a noon meal and the stove threw off a welcomed warmth against the chilly air from the still-open front door.

Mom hugged Kathy as a greeting, and Kathy awkwardly returned the gesture. Kathy liked her space, but Mom tended to hug everyone. A misunderstood signal, perhaps, but that was unimportant right now.

As I hugged Mom, the pit of my stomach turned. It had been a week since I had seen her. She was smiling but more frail and thinner than I imagined she would be.

We sat down to a lunch of chili and homemade bread, but I noticed Mom's bowl was bare. She sat there gaunt and wide-eyed, sipping her water and nibbling at her crackers. Only the clinking of the silverware against bowls of chili broke the silence. I looked at my sister, Mary, and her husband, Tim, and realized how much had changed in a week.

In his overalls, my dad sat subdued at one end of the table, hardly saying a word until he learned Kathy worked at Northland Breeders.

"Narrows Valley Brown Swiss!" Kathy flashed her Jessica Lange smile and ran her fingers through her honey-blonde hair. "We have one of your bulls in our stud."

"They bought him three years ago from us," Dad proudly replied. The frown on his white forehead, which was always protected from the sun by his hat, had temporarily disappeared.

"I really admire what Jim has accomplished," Kathy again broke the silence. "He's become my mentor at work."

" . . . Our big brother," Mary chimed in, chuckling. "I guess that's sort of like being a mentor."

"Big brothers can be a pain, too," I said. "Remember when I used to correct Paul's themes in college? Big mistake."

"Being the oldest is not easy," Kathy agreed. "I have a younger sister and brother, and I can't believe what they get away with that I could have never done at their age."

"You just get worn down after the third and fourth kid," Mom said with a weak smile.

A trip to the home farm was giving both of us what we needed. For Kathy, it was something different to do during what she considered a backwater time in her life. Perhaps quasi-dating an older man with a disability who grew up in rural Wisconsin was also a partial atonement for her life of privilege in Milwaukee. And the rebellious, liberal side of her relished a challenge to convention.

For me it was a chance to show my family I could establish an adult relationship with an attractive, intelligent woman. Yes, I had a good friend in Kathy. No, a friendship between a man and woman did not always have to lead to romance—a concept not easily understood in rural Wisconsin. Was I interested in developing a romantic relationship with Kathy? Of course. But, that was still an open question. I was still growing. I was going to be all right.

We had come in separate cars. It was safer that way. It proved our independence. It showed we were not a couple.

After lunch Kathy and I walked slowly down the farmstead's driveway. We crossed the road and tramped across a field of tangled cornstalks toward a hill of red-tinged oaks. Swinging my crutches sideways to maintain my balance while walking across the rows, I occasionally caught some of the cornstalks left by the corn picker. I would stop, untangle my crutches, and move on.

"Nice family," Kathy said in a muse, as the sun began to take the chill out of the fall air. "I really like your mom."

"She's gone downhill quite a bit during this last week," I replied, almost to myself. "She's not eating much at all. She used to like food so much."

As we walked back to the house, high, thin clouds began to move in, and the air became chilly. Kathy left, and I went into the house to spend time with Mom, who was sitting in her favorite chair by the window with a knitted shawl around her arms.

"Good to have Kathy come out. I watched you two go all the way across that field," she said slowly. "It takes someone special to take the time to walk with you like that."

"I'm sure she didn't mind. It was just so nice out."

"How long have you known Kathy?"

"About a year. It's nothing serious," I emphasized. "We're just good friends."

Growing Space

Life can only be understood backwards, but it must be lived forwards.

—Soren Kierkegaard
Life

"Why does your tree do so well?" Liz, Sam Jansen's administrative assistant, asked as she helped me pack the last of my books from the overhead bins above my desk.

My weeping fig tree was not weeping at all. Thick with dark, green leaves, its branches commanded one corner of my office, and, over the years, I had to turn the tree occasionally so it would not invade the space normally belonging to my visitors who sat on the window side of my circular conference table.

"The secret is in the rocks," I confided to Liz. "And having a large enough pot. The roots need growing space."

Sheila, my sole associate in the communications department at the time, and I had purchased the tree from a local flower shop when Sam first became president in 1977. It was such a little thing.

But my mom came over from the farm one night and helped us re-pot it. She poured a small bag of white rock into the bottom of the pot, which looked huge at the time. It took three big bags of potting soil to fill it up.

"And you haven't done anything to it since then?" Liz asked again.

"Not really," I replied. "Just added some soil once in a while, watered regularly, and kept turning it ever so often to give each branch a chance at the sun."

It was March 31, 1994, the day I retired from my job. After twenty-eight years with the same organization and seventeen years with the same weeping fig tree providing a softer touch to my office, I had no feeling of remorse or loss. I was intent in building a second career with a little more breathing space for myself.

I had thought about transferring the fig tree to the new home Pam, my wife, and I had built in 1985, but somehow we never found the right spot for it. By that time, it was six feet tall and had branches spanning a diameter of more than five feet. It would have been difficult to move.

Somehow it seemed right to have it in my office because it was a daily reminder of who I was.

My parents had been dairy farmers all their lives—and members of one of the thirty predecessor cooperatives which had consolidated over the years to form Heartland Dairies.

As a dairy farmer's wife, Mom had not only helped our family milk registered Brown Swiss twice each day for nearly thirty-five years but also kept the records and pedigrees of all of the animals in our barn.

With the same diligence, she had nurtured her children, fostering a self-confidence in each one as we completed grade school and high school and graduated from college.

"You make us proud," she would say privately to each one of us. It was her way of giving us growing space. She wanted us to feel special, to recognize the unique qualities we had within ourselves and the opportunities we had to share those qualities with others. Yet, she knew we would each encounter setbacks and discouragement along the way that would test that self-confidence. As I look back, I could see she was especially concerned about how I would handle my disability as I grew into adulthood.

As a seven-year-old, I would cry in front of a different set of passengers every Monday morning as I boarded a Greyhound bus at Spring Green for a week at orthopedic school and my weekday second parents in Madison. I dreaded the uncertainty of another week away from home.

But, at thirteen, I dreaded coming back home from Madison to face the unforeseeable difficulties of attending a local high school.

And I remember crying in front of my family at eighteen because I could feel the enormous pressure of making it as the firstborn to enter college. I questioned whether I was up to dealing with all that could possibly go wrong.

Would I be able to preserve my self-esteem as I faced—from some—rejection, ridicule, and scorn? Would my constructive self-image propel me into new opportunities of which I had not yet dreamed?

"Sam can have the tree," I finally said to Liz, as I turned out the lights in my now-bare office and stepped next door to glance in at Sam's scraggly weeping fig, which had been struggling for survival since the mid 1980s.

"He'll appreciate that," She replied. "His looks so awful. We haven't been able to do much with it."

Putting the tree into Sam's office was more appropriate—and better for it. His corner office faced the west and south, so it would receive both the morning and afternoon sun and welcome both overalled dairy farmer and dark-suited businessman as they walked in to greet him.

The right legacy, I thought, as I walked through the executive wing of the office one last time. The tree was well-established, and the rocks in the bottom of the pot were giving the roots just the right drainage.

Back on Track

You gain strength, courage, and confidence by every experience in which you really stop to look fear in the face.

—Eleanor Roosevelt
You Learn by Living

I nudged Pam as the choir finished its anthem. It was time for Pam to read. I couldn't understand why she was not walking up to the altar.

Finally, Pam stood. But before taking a step out of the pew, she sat down again beside me. I looked up and saw Susan at the lectern. She had remained at the front of the church after singing with the choir and promptly read the lesson. I didn't dare look at Pam, for I could feel her consternation next to me.

She checked the Sunday bulletin again, and there it was in black and white. Pam Hasse, 10:30 service, lector.

With ease, Susan finished reading the second lesson in perfect diction and rhythm. I grabbed a quick glance at Pam's crestfallen face. Her jaw was clenched tightly. Her eyes, which could dance with delight and detachment, had grown vacant, withdrawn, and cold beneath her newly permed hair. Her face had become ashen, highlighting her pink blush lipstick.

It was as if she were dying in her new chartreuse outfit. I reached for her hand, but she withdrew it as though she had touched a hot stove.

I wanted to hug her, to comfort her, but it was not appropriate, for we were sitting in the front pew. So I sat there, knowing I was in the company of another fragile human being who was withdrawing to the point where she didn't want my understanding touch.

In my mind I kept searching for an explanation of what had happened as the minister gave his sermon. Pam, also not listening, stared blankly at her feet.

We had left home early for the 10:30 service because Pam, when she is lector, always likes to make sure the lessons she is about to read are indeed on the lectern. At 10:00, I turned on the car radio so we could listen to the first part of the taped broadcast of the 8:15 service.

"Be sure to pay close attention to our first lesson in Deuteronomy," Pastor Higgens said in his opening remarks of the rebroadcast. "Today's sermon is based on that reading."

"Deuteronomy?" Pam repeated in disbelief. "Did I get the wrong lesson?" She quickly looked it up. "No, they must have changed lessons!"

"That's OK," I assured her. "When we get there, just read through the stuff a couple of times to yourself. You've got time."

"I'll just read it," she said disappointedly. "I won't be able to look up at the congregation."

"That's right," I added, always giving too much advice. "Just read it slowly."

But I knew that's not how she wanted things to go. In her mind, she was not prepared. Since she has total loss of hearing in her left ear, she was in the habit of reading and rereading the lessons aloud at home for perhaps a dozen times during the course of the week before her scheduled reading. She worked hard to get the right pronunciation, pace, and emphasis.

Sometimes, we both struggled with words such as "thwart" and "Zion." I would try to pronounce them how I thought they should sound, but they would invariably come out of my mouth warped and wooden due to my cerebral palsy. Pam would repeat how she was hearing them, and after several attempts, we usually came to a close "approximation" of what most people would recognize as normal speech.

By Friday, she would usually tell me, "I've got it down."

And by that time we would have had extended discussions about what the passage meant and how it complemented the verses before and after it. Only a few weeks before, Pastor Higgens had commented about the feeling Pam put into her readings, as though she really felt the Scripture's power and meaning.

I was so proud of her. Reading in front of a group was something I still personally feared due to my speech difficulties. She was doing so well with something I could not comfortably do myself.

Just ten years before, Pam could not read in front of a group, either. She would giggle inappropriately in what seemed like an uncontrollable escape from the tension of taking center stage in front of even a few people.

After we married, we both took a Dale Carnegie course about effective human relations and public speaking, and that experience broke Pam's giggling habit.

As we entered the sanctuary, I was hoping this mixup in scriptural readings would not shatter Pam's growing self-confidence. She retrieved a copy of the readings from the lectern before the service and came down the aisle to join me in the pew. Quickly she read through the passages. She understood them. They were not difficult.

"How do you pronounce this word?" she suddenly asked.

"*A-ra-mean,*" I repeated slowly to myself. I wasn't sure. We checked the pew Bible. No pronunciation help.

I whispered in her "good" ear, "It's either *Ar-a-mean* or *Ara-me-an.*"

With four vowels in one word, my rendition of *Aramean* kept coming out as *Ara-mean-i-an* in Pam's ears. Finally, I suggested she go check the word with Pastor Higgens. There was still time, and she did.

"It's *Ara-me-an,*" she said when she came back to our pew. She was confident, nervous but prepared.

Yet, during the service Susan unexpectedly took Pam's place in reading the lessons.

"I want to go," Pam promptly urged as soon as the service ended. I could see the anger and disappointment boil within her. We sneaked out the side entrance and made it to our car without talking to anyone.

"What happened?" I asked as soon as we were in the car, knowing she still did not want to be hugged.

"I know what happened," she replied tartly. "Pastor Higgens asked Susan to read for me because he thought I couldn't do it."

"Why?" I asked in disbelief. "Did you ask him to have someone read for you?"

"No, I just mentioned that the church office had switched lessons sometime during the week, and I didn't know how to pronounce *Aramean*. It was an easy reading. I could have done it. I should have had the option of reading it, since I knew I could do it. He didn't tell me he was going to ask Susan to read for me."

"You sure you didn't hear him ask you that?"

"No-o-o-o! I know what I said and what he said! I just needed help with that one word," Pam exploded. "I don't feel like reading anymore."

It was something I had hoped I would never hear Pam say, but she said it repeatedly as she brewed about it on Monday and Tuesday. And I resisted the temptation of saying, "You want to quit reading because you're afraid you'll get rejected again."

Instead, I let her diffuse her anger. Giving each other space is one of the rituals we like to say we practice now and then—just as we both actively seek each other's appraisal and approval to the point of childishness when either one of us successfully accomplishes a difficult task.

By Wednesday her anger was gone. On Thursday she called the church office to reconfirm the next weekend's readings. By coincidence or divine intervention, she had signed up two months before to be lector at the next Saturday night service.

On Friday morning, I heard her practice her reading in the kitchen as I came out of the shower.

And she did just fine at Saturday night's service.

How Does Gaining Self-Assurance Apply to Your Situation?

1. How can you make your "self-talk" constructive instead of destructive?

2. In what ways are you trying to overcompensate for a range of personal imperfections with an unneeded pursuit of perfection in one or more skills?

3. What incidents show you can recognize and accept, with amusement instead of anger, deception both on an individual and cultural level?

4. Under what circumstances have you mustered the courage to uncover and accept your true motives?

5. What instances can you cite to show you recognized that making an unexpected change would further your personal growth?

6. Under what circumstances can perseverence build your self-confidence?

Chapter 2

Achieving Self-Sufficiency

On the Darker Side of Brilliance

We should not pretend to understand the world only by the intellect; we apprehend it just as much by feeling.

—Carl Jung
Psychological Types

I slumped lower into my seat, trying not to kick my crutches on the floor and draw attention to myself and disturb the class with the clank of tubular aluminum against hardwood.

Professor Brown began reading aloud the paper I had submitted two days before for my Journalism 101 course. He read the first paragraph without commitment, and I quickly prepared myself for the worst.

After all, he was a legend as a reporter for *Newsweek.* I had already visualized what it must have been like to dictate his story quickly, paragraph by paragraph, from scribbled notes over a phone from Seoul to New York during the Korean War.

Our assignment had been to write an opinion piece, and I didn't understand why he had picked my paper to read to the class. He hadn't shared the writings of anyone in the class before.

It was a ragtag course the scope of which I still did not fully understand, even though the first six-weeks' exam was getting dangerously close.

In hindsight, I guess it was an introductory journalism class to sort out those of us with journalistic tendencies (potential) and the others who would do better in the School of Business or Animal Husbandry.

"Paragraph," Professor Brown said slowly.

"'As I hoppled toward the bus, I noticed a *George-Wallace-For-President* sign in the store-front window.'"

Not until that moment did I realize what I had done. My speech sometimes switches the "bb" sound with "pp," and, in repeating the sentence to myself, I had inadvertently typed "hoppled" instead of "hobbled."

"Let's stop for a moment right here. Do you see anything unusual about that sentence?"

The silence was awkward.

"'Hoppled'," he answered. His mustache twitched, and I squirmed. "Isn't that a creative way of describing the way a person would proceed in catching a bus?"

"It was a mistake," I silently repeated to myself in disbelief and wondered how many in the class realized it was a typo. I looked around the room. No one was smiling.

My piece went on to repeat some of George Wallace's favorite statements about "conservatizing this country." It was October, 1963, and the shocking TV news reports about the demonstrations and riots in Birmingham, Alabama disturbed me.

The issue of states' versus federal government's rights didn't particularly appeal to me. Yet, Wallace's most graphic question kept popping up in my mind: "Do you know what those liberal Washington bureaucrats carry in their black briefcases? Peanut-butter sandwiches."

"Do you know what every Negro has in his wallet?" I had Wallace asking in my paper. "An ACLU card."

George Wallace's drive as a candidate for the presidency in the 1964 elections had already begun on the University of Wisconsin campus in Madison. He was playing on my prejudices—and those of heartland America— but I didn't realize it.

As I look back, my essay reflected how naive I was about bigotry in this country when I was twenty and a junior in college.

"Some white Southern politicians often feel inferior to their Washington counterparts from other parts of the country," I observed in my essay. "So, why should they be faulted for using the same putdowns they've endured to divide a minority population back home that threatens to tear this country apart?"

As Professor Brown finished reading my paper, he didn't use my name.

"Isn't that clever?" he asked rhetorically, nodding his head in agreement with himself. He never looked at me. The class was again silent.

"Exposing the bigotry of George Wallace by using parody and paradox," Brown concluded, evidently using my paper as an illustration of creative writing.

I was still waiting for the balloon to burst. I did not mean to write a parody. I thought George Wallace had some legitimate observations and thought they needed to be repeated in the liberal environment of the Madison campus.

Still, the balloon did not burst. He was serious. No class discussion.

I felt uncomfortable and never discussed my paper with him. Perhaps I should have and removed the tinge of paternalism I still feel thirty years later as I remember Professor Brown and Journalism 101.

The Back Door Into Adulthood

So our self-feeling in this world depends entirely on what we back ourselves to be and do.

—William James
The Principles of Psychology

The last time I referred to myself as "Jimmy" was in the fourth grade, and it never cropped up all the way through high school and college.

But when I entered the workforce after college, I noticed the tendency among my superiors to call me "Jimmy," even though I clearly signed my letters "James R. Hasse," and the masthead of our company newsletter displayed the line, "Jim Hasse, Editor."

As an ongoing amusement among the staff people in my department, they started tracking who within our organization called me, "Jim," and who called me, "Jimmy." We found the "Jimmy" people fell into two camps: the truly unenlightened and the condescending.

I must admit I have met very few condescenders in rural America.

Since my staff and I classified most of our "Jimmy" people as unenlightened, I gave the issue only a passing thought. Some things were worth fighting for, and some were not. I had bigger fish to fry.

It was the early 1970s. I was making headway in my job—getting things accomplished for the organization that I thought needed to get done, challenging management in a patient way to change ever so slightly into a more participative mode of management.

Then Jimmy Carter went to Washington. Our nation recaptured some hope and needed self-renewal after the dark days of Watergate. As a candidate, he managed to symbolize a fresh approach to politics that quickly evaporated after two years in office. I sadly watched his credibility slip away on the world stage as well as at home after the Sadat-Begin agreement, probably the high point of his presidency.

Why did that happen? Yes, he was an honest, principled man, but he lacked charisma and experience in wielding the worldly ways of power.

And he lacked something else: a first name that is credible in our culture (or, at least, in the isolated ranks of Washington, where condescension is one of the tools in the fine art of politics).

During Carter's fall from favor with the American public, I began to realize how "Jimmy" could also be patronizing in my case as well.

Called "Jimmy" and tagged as "crippled" was a double whammy, reinforcing long-established stereotypes that don't die easily in a rural area.

That really didn't become clear to me until my friend, Shauna, challenged me to become more assertive about the matter.

A single parent of two grade schoolers, Shauna was an accomplished musician and intellectually astute. She also happened to be overweight.

"Esther kept calling me 'Shaunie,' and I finally called her on it," she explained. "You've got to do the same."

But I found it difficult to correct people in person, and, to this day, I've never challenged anyone by simply and directly saying, "I prefer to be called 'Jim'."

Lacking that assertiveness at the time, I took the back-door approach instead. As I gained more visibility through professional accomplishments, I became the subject of several newspaper profiles about how "a man with disability makes good."

Inevitably, the question would always come with every interview, "What would you change in how people relate to you as a person with a disability?"

Every chance I had I used the "Jimmy" example, replying to a trite question with a trite answer. It slowly worked. The media helped me say, "I'm not a 'Jimmy' anymore." Today, the "Jimmy" people are either reformed or out of my circle of contacts.

Nevertheless, for me to find a way to take my personal step into adulthood took years—the same journey someone named Howie, Donnie or Pammy as a child normally learns to take much earlier in life.

A Puzzle for Christmas

One can know nothing of giving anything that is worthy to give unless one also knows how to take.

—Havelock Ellis

Little Essays of Love and Virtue

As I look back, I should have been more perceptive and taken the five bucks. But I wouldn't have felt good about it.

Two weeks before Christmas Pam and I were doing our version of "power shopping." Coming through the K-Mart entrance, we saw a wheelchair for customer use. Pam grabbed it and rolled it to me.

I flopped into the chair and parked my crutches across my lap. We took off for the toy department with Pam pushing me through the narrow, cluttered aisles.

We got to the toys and started browsing among the games and puzzles. I felt (and probably looked) bewildered.

Our niece was five and into puzzles. "What can you get a kid who sees all those cool graphics on TV?" I asked Pam, expecting no answer. "Even if I think it's fun, she'll probably be bored with it. I have no idea what it's like to be five years old nowadays."

It was then that I became aware of an old man, gray and thin, behind us.

He tottered up to me with a five-dollar bill in his hand and offered it to me. "Here take this," he urged, "and have a Merry Christmas."

"No, that's OK," I said in a knee-jerk reaction. "Thanks, anyway."

Independence. Charity. My gut reaction: They don't go together.

He persisted. "Here," he offered the bill to Pam. "Take it."

"No, you keep it," Pam replied, gently but firmly. "We don't need it. Thank you."

We wheeled to the next aisle, trying to put some space between us and the old man.

Finally, out of his sight, we giggled because we had again been confronted with the common perception that a person with a disability is in financial need—that somehow a handout can help.

We giggled out of haughtiness, too, because we knew we probably were much better off financially than he was. And we giggled out of pride because we knew we were unusual—that a lot of people with disabilities are in need.

When we got home, though, we started thinking more about the old man.

"We probably should have taken the money," Pam finally said, cornering me in the kitchen.

"Why?" I asked. "It would have reinforced his idea of how he can help. And that's not true in many cases."

"Look at it from his point of view," Pam countered. "He was offering help to a real, live person—probably the only way he knew how to help."

"It would have been dishonest, honey," I emphasized, risking a quick glance into her hazel eyes. "I just wouldn't have felt right about taking it."

Long pause.

"We rejected a gift," she finally said stiffly. "If that's not contempt, I don't know what is."

Long pause.

She had me.

Cupping my tight jaw in both palms, I slumped over the kitchen table and used both of my elbows as props. "It'll probably never happen again," I assured her.

So far, it hasn't. If it ever does, I'll probably take the money and still not feel good about it.

Ripe for Revolution

After all, there is but one race—humanity.

—George Moore
The Bending of the Bough

"Russell," Mr. Johansson called to one of the field hands, "show the people here how you watch to make sure the water system is working."

Russell, a slight black man in a floppy straw hat, nervously grinned at the bulky farmer, who stood beaming with a fist wrapped around each suspender which held his khaki slacks above his broad belly. The seven-foot cornstalks rustled in the hot Rhodesian wind.

"Go up!" Mr. Johansson commanded. He looked back apologetically at our group of fifteen agri-business people from Wisconsin. "Russell's a little shy."

Russell shimmied up the twelve-foot pole at the edge of the cornfield and positioned himself on the crude seat which crowned the pole's top. He took off his hat and awkwardly placed the four fingers of his right hand against his forehead in a salute.

He then slowly moved his head from right to left and left to right, as if surveying every section of pipe in the irrigation system. I nervously watched the faces within our group for some sign of the embarrassment I felt, but I couldn't tell what my fellow travelers were thinking.

Russell continued the demonstration until Mr. Johansson interrupted with an uproarious laugh that shook his pink, clean-shaven jowls and deepened the lines around his blue eyes. "You can come down now," he ordered.

Carla, our Rhodesian guide, was a tall, spindly lady with short, blonde hair and a British accent. She stood next to Mr. Johannson and giggled as Russell slid down the pole.

"Six more weeks, and it'll be ripe," Mr. Johansson estimated, referring to his corn crop. "It usually gets dry in August, so we have to irrigate."

I pushed the red soil with my left crutch tip. It was dry and didn't seem as fertile as the deep brown loam we had back home. As I swaggered to the bus with the usual wide swoops I perform with my crutches while walking, I kicked up the red dust. The shiny black shoes I had put on that morning were now coated with a red layer of soil. I kicked both shoes against the bus's front tire to free them of the dust. But they didn't look any better.

Our bus driver, who hadn't said a word all morning, started the engine and closed the door when the last members of our group, Mr. Johansson and Carla, came aboard. He put the bus into reverse and nervously checked both side mirrors as he slowly backed out of the cornfield. Sitting behind the driver, I saw beads of sweat form on his black neck as the bus slowly inched backwards.

We finally got to an opening where the bus could make a Y-turn and proceed out of the field. The driver tugged at the steering wheel with both of his thick hands, trying to turn a sharp right, but the bus shimmied and stalled. He again started the engine and gunned it to make sure it was running properly. We backed to the right in spurts.

Carla, standing in the aisle of the bus, gave a loud sigh of disgust. "I don't know what the problem is," she said sarcastically with a shrug to the group, as though the driver couldn't hear her. "Some of these drivers they give us . . . "

Even though she was educated in England with a degree in economics, she obviously didn't know how difficult it was to turn a heavy bus around without power steering in a dusty field. Mr. Johansson silently stood next to her. They held on to the center pole but swayed with each jerk.

Earlier that morning, as our group had met the Johansson family outside of their white, two-story farmhouse, Rod, the leader of our group, introduced each one of us.

"And, finally, this is Jim Hasse, who is communication director for one of our largest dairy co-ops in Wisconsin," I heard Rod emphasize.

"Good morning," I greeted Mr. Johansson, acknowledging the introduction.

Mr. Johansson's eyes ran the full length of my crutches but never looked me in the face. He said nothing to me. Instead, he proceeded to describe his farm, which totaled 1,000 acres of cropland and an extensive hog operation.

Our first stop was the hog operation, where we met Willie, a graying black man with a limp and quick smile, who was tending the hogs.

"Willie's learning how to take care of our hogs," Mr. Johansson told our group. "Aren't you, Willie?"

"Yes, sir," replied Willie breathlessly as he wrestled with a boar he brought out of the hog barn to show to our group. Sort of like an apprenticeship, I told myself. Wasn't that unusual for a man who was perhaps in his sixties?

"We have our own school for the children on our farm," Mr. Johansson pointed out as we rode back to the Johansson farmhouse later that morning. "Right here on the corner. We have about twenty kids."

The unpainted frame building was perhaps 20 by 30 feet. Its door stood halfway open, and the two windows on each side of the door didn't have panes in them. The sun shone through the door at the bare, wood floor. I saw no desks.

Before we reached the farmhouse, our bus passed a road crew of prisoners, all black. I was surprised to see not one white man was in the group. Then I reminded myself that the Rhodesian population, ruled by a slim minority of whites, was ninety percent black. Rhodesia was one of the few remaining white-ruled countries in Africa.

Stan, one of the dairy farmers in our group, asked Mr. Johansson about the recent reports of social unrest in the country.

"There can be attacks by night," Mr. Johansson admitted. "We have to be careful after dark. They're communist-inspired uprisings."

Our group again fell silent. It was 1973, seven years before white Rhodesia became black Zimbabwe. I marveled at the alleged ability of communist conspirators to infiltrate movements around the world—from the civil rights marches in America and the civil wars of Central America to uprisings in Ethiopia and Rhodesia. They must have been busy folks.

"My grandfather started farming this country in 1880," Mr. Johansson offered. "We know how to farm this land. If the blacks take over, it'll be a terrible thing for this country. They don't have the skills to run it."

I cringed but knew that argument probably made sense to some in our group.

Back at the hotel in Salisbury, we walked into the lobby, windblown and dusty. The doorman was a white person, perhaps in his fifties and barely three feet tall. Carla, who towered over the little man as she entered the lobby, temporarily joined some of the wives of our group under the lobby's chandelier.

"Isn't he cute?" I heard her remark in a giggle as she watched the doorman. It was as if she were talking about someone's pet dog. She received no response from the others.

I went up to my room disappointed and discouraged by the paternalism and mendacity I had both felt and observed that day. My shoes were still red with the dust from the fields, and I carefully brushed them off in the bathroom. But, they still looked grungy at the dinner party we had with the Johanssons at the hotel that night.

Rejections Justified

He who excuses himself accuses himself.

—Gabriel Meurier
Tresor des Sentences

"This is not going to work out," Carol said matter-of-factly. Sitting across from me at the tear-shaped breakfast bar in my condo, she took another sip of her coffee, shifted her weight in the beige chair and folded her arms across her pink robe.

I felt the muscles in my forearms and in the calves of my legs stiffen.

"What do you mean?" I asked in a sloppy string of five raspy vowels that even sounded strange to me. I didn't want to hear the answer.

"I'm moving back to Tennessee," she announced. Her brown eyes unblinkingly met mine before they sank into her coffee cup. She again looked up at me in the peaceful quiet of the dark winter morning. I could see in them her disappointment and conviction.

"Why?"

"Because that's where I belong. I moved away fifteen years ago because I had to. But now I'm my own person. I can deal with Mom's drinking."

Dressed in a white polo shirt and blue jeans, I sat back in my chair and sipped my orange juice from a tall glass my gnarled hands had learned to handle. Carol's announcement was another of her strange changes in direction that I had come to anticipate after knowing her for only six months.

Through Carol, I had learned about serendipidity, but too many side trips distracted me. I needed a companion who had a clear direction of where she wanted to go. And it would be nice if that direction dovetailed with mine.

Maybe it was her divorce. But that was two years ago. Carol was acting like a frightened rabbit that finally escapes into the taller grass of an undeveloped lot after venturing onto a closely clipped suburban lawn and encountering a deck party of noisy neighbors.

A solid marriage, good friends, a quiet home, and a secure job—that was my dream. And I had a promising job, the first ticket to that future.

"You're so placid," she finally added. "You're so weak."

"What do you mean?" I asked blankly, trying to hide my rejection of her irrational conclusions, her harsh charges, her banal past in the lucid stillness of the morning.

"I mean you have no passion . . . ," she slowly said, sad and resentful. Her right hand left the coffee cup and did a deliberate, controlled flip, as if trying to communicate what she couldn't put into words.

"Passion for what?" I demanded, uncomfortably surprised she had picked on a feeling I had not really explored before. What was passion, anyway?

"Passion for me!" Carol blurted out. "Passion for what I stand for! Passion for what I've been through!"

For the first time, I saw her eyes grow sharp, her cheeks draw taut and her upper lip curl into an ugly snarl—the stance she perhaps had to sometimes take as a nursing supervisor for a metropolitan hospital. "And you don't make decisions."

"What do you mean, I don't make decisions?" I shouted in flat consonants. "How do you think I got to where I am today?"

"Decisions about us—that's what I mean!" she said curtly, almost under her breath.

"How can I leave a good job and go to Tennessee with you?" I said, resorting to the same question I had posed in previous arguments about the issue. "What about my career? Why should I start over?"

"That's what I mean!" Carol said, again raising her voice and flinging the backside of her hand toward me with all four fingers spread apart. "No passion! No decision!"

"Carol, I need you!" I heard myself saying, knowing I was giving in to that buried longing everyone has for a surrogate mother but suppresses as too childish for the adult world. Tears ran down my face. It was not so much that I needed Carol. I grieved for my vulnerability and loneliness, exposing a self-pity I didn't know I had.

I had broken the promise I had made to myself as a person with a disability never to admit I needed the emotional support of another person, a spouse or a friend. I cussed myself for using the code word, "need," that the women's movement had loaded with connotations of weakness and chauvinism.

"See!" Carol snapped. "That's what worries me. I don't want to be your crutch."

"I don't want you to become my crutch!" I shot back through my tears, disappointed that she, like so many others during the early '80s, were not separating emotional and psychological dependency from spiritual and intellectual needs. "That's the last thing I would want to happen!"

"I just can't see myself going through the rest of my life with someone on crutches," she said more calmly. "The other day I was trying to imagine what it would be like—always moving so slowly . . . "

"I thought we had gotten beyond that," I broke in, flinching under the impersonal tone of her analysis.

"No, we haven't," She said quietly. "I don't know what you're going to do. Where are you going to find—around here—someone like me?"

Playing the Pauper

The easiest person to deceive is one's own self.

—Edward Bulwer-Lytton
The Disowned

"I've got 84 cents," I sheepishly told the fellow in a Hardee's shirt behind the counter. "What can I buy for that?" It was 2:30 in the afternoon. My stomach felt hollow. I needed some cholesterol and caffeine to keep me going.

His name badge read, "Ned," and it hung crookedly from the pocket of his shirt, which was too big for his slender frame. He glanced awkwardly at my crutches, turned around and looked at the menu overhead. "Well, there's the 59-cent cheeseburger," he said in a squeaky voice. "And that's about all . . . "

Garish menu boards always seem confusing to me. "What's a carton of white milk?"

"Forty-nine cents."

Milk is expensive, I thought.

"How about a small Coke?" I mumbled, thinking that would be cheaper.

"Fifty-nine cents."

Maybe milk is not such a bad deal. "Just give me the

cheeseburger," I finally said, satisfied that it would get me through the afternoon.

"What does he want?" I overheard Gert quietly ask Ned as she suddenly appeared behind the counter. She wore thick bifocals and a floppy cap over her gray hair.

"Cheeseburger and milk," he whispered through the side of his mouth, as though I couldn't hear him or that I was unaware of what Gert had asked. "He's only got 84 cents."

"Give it to him," she ordered in a matronly manner that, at the same time, maintained her aloofness. "I'll pick up the difference."

"How do I . . . ?" Ned, apparently new at the computer, started to ask.

"I'll take care of it later," Gert insisted as she checked the coffee pot on the back counter.

He slapped the pre-wrapped cheeseburger and the milk carton on a tray. I gave him the 84 cents I had in the palm of my hand.

"I'll bring it out to the table for you," Gert offered. So I shimmied over to the nearest table and plopped down into the chair. My crutches hit the floor with a clank. This was not the right thing to do—but so what? I was entitled to a bit of charity now and then.

Gert came over with my tray. "Thank you," I said, trying to sound appreciative and intelligent at the same time.

"That's OK," she assured me, speaking louder and more distinctly than she needed to. "You have a nice lunch now."

She probably thought she understood my situation, but she didn't. It was all an accidental fabrication that looked real. The circumstances—and the perceptions—had just fallen into place, and instead of overriding the impressions I stood by and watched them play out.

Anyway, it was too silly and irrational to explain to a stranger. For the first time in my life, the perception that I, as a person with a disability, was jobless and didn't have the cash for a decent meal had become a reality.

Being jobless was not entirely right, though. I had just retired from a twenty-eight-year career in public relations for a Fortune 500 company and was beginning to feel the trauma in establishing my own consulting business.

And I had credit cards. I had paid for a business lunch just two hours before with my MasterCard. But I had not eaten much of my crab salad. I had been absorbed instead in taking notes of the intriguing ideas my partner had for helping college seniors with disabilities prepare for the job market.

So just sixty miles later I was hungry and had stopped for a quick sandwich—only to discover I had left home that morning in my drive to Milwaukee without cash. A quick check of the usual places for random change in my car only yielded 84 cents.

I left my coat and tie in the car, buoyed by the confidence I had enough to buy something to drink and the 59-cent cheeseburger promoted on the marquee above the disabled parking stall just outside the front door.

Coming up short for cash hadn't happened to me before. For the moment, I amused myself in shallow self-pity and understood, perhaps for the first time, what it meant to tell myself, "I'm entitled." It was, after all, harmless, anonymous, and inconsequential. I received the milk—and energy—I needed for the two-hour drive home. I surprised myself by accepting the handout without shame.

Now I could see that I was the center of attention for the crew in the mostly vacant restaurant. Quick glances shot in my direction from over the plastic greenery and behind the gaudy counter. I left my tray at the table and went to the men's room, hoping I could quietly sneak out afterwards without the employees seeing me.

I came out of the restroom, letting my crutches slide silently on the floor, trying not to draw attention. But near the entrance I met Gert, mopping the floor with wide swipes. Ned was cleaning off the tables.

"Thanks again," I said pleasantly, as I staggered to the door, using one crutch and then the other to pull me across the floor as fast as I could.

"That's OK," Gert replied loudly.

My normally easy gait became jerky. Ned opened the door for me, and I went out with extra difficulty. It seemed as though I took five minutes to find my keys, unlock the front door, and climb into my 1990 Maxima. As I drove out of the parking lot, Gert and Ned were still standing there, watching me—she with the mop in her hand and he with a stack of trays.

Troubled Tribute

Life is a continual struggle to justify the discrepancy between our own perceptions and those of others about who we are.

—Anonymous

I saw my mother-in-law rise to her feet at the table right in front of the podium as soon as the applause began. She stood there alone, a smile on her face, looking at me and clapping for a long three seconds—out of love and pride—before others, here and there in the large banquet hall, began to pop up to their feet. Then, the whole banquet hall gave me a standing ovation.

Until then, I was comfortable receiving the Co-op Builder Award during the twenty-fifth annual meeting of the Wisconsin Federation of Cooperatives in Madison.

But as I gingerly stabbed each of the steps leading off the riser with my crutches to get a sure footing for my return to my family's banquet table, my stomach became queasy. Otto and Marian Christopherson, two other Co-op Builder recipients who accepted their awards before I came on stage, hadn't received a standing ovation. Why should I?

Then two more Co-op Builder recipients appeared before the banquet crowd of three hundred people—Julian

Warren, a strong business leader who had served as chairman of the board for several cooperatives during the last thirty years, and Damon Szymanski, an outstanding dairy farmer and volunteer who had spearheaded twenty-five projects to advise agricultural and cooperative leaders in Eastern Europe and the former Soviet Union. They did not receive standing ovations. So why should I?

Maybe I don't understand the unspoken rules of a standing ovation. I suspect that once there are at least five people on their feet who are clapping enthusiastically in an audience of a couple hundred people, a standing ovation is in the making.

Every time I see at least five people standing and clapping at the end of a play or a concert—and I'm still sitting—I feel guilty. Was the performance that good? I just assume the five people are experts and know a superb performance when they see one. So I stand and join them. Yes, the performance was special.

To me, the most intriguing performer of our evening was Damon, who had used his knowledge of dairy cooperatives and the Polish language to help foster economic development in Poland on a volunteer basis. Didn't that dedication deserve a standing ovation?

The program brochure for the awards banquet summarized the accomplishments of each recipient. "Jim's primary skill is communications," it read, "and, while working with a severe speech handicap, he has reached the pinnacle of his profession through his writing and through coaching other people."

All five of us award winners were recognized that night for our leadership and our contributions to the cooperative movement in Wisconsin. Each of us took a different path, based on our skills and vocation, in achieving our goals.

And in the process we each had taken advantage of our strengths and had overcome our weaknesses.

So why should a man with crutches and a speech difficulty receive special recognition with a standing ovation? The other honorees probably had gone through struggles just as real but not as apparent as I had.

Warren could have been suffering from painful bunions for the last twenty years—bunions that could have made him irritable. Yet, no one could have known for sure because he would have had the fortitude to overcome that grouchiness.

Instead, Warren developed the reputation for effectively fostering the teamwork that made him successful as a board chairman of several cooperatives.

For all we knew, Damon could have had a fear of flying. He could have quietly fought a panic every time he flew to meet with his co-op counterparts in Eastern Europe.

The ovation actually negated the commonality I had with the other four Co-op Builders. I was separated from the group as special, when, in reality, all five of us were special.

How Does Achieving Self-Sufficiency Apply to Your Situation?

1. How can you effectively prevent the paternalism you can probably expect in your situation from damaging your self-image?

2. What do you do about situations that have little consequence in the eyes of others but reinforce stereotypes about you that you are trying to overcome?

3. How do you project your image about how you want to come across in the eyes of others in your personal relationships and casual acquaintances?

4. How have you become a student of stereotyping in your particular community, and how do you use those insights to your advantage?

5. How do you focus on what you need psychologically, emotionally, spiritually, and physically in personal relationships so you can avoid using superficial differences as excuses for rejection?

6. What are the limits beyond which you cannot trust your preconceived notions about how you'll react in an unusual situation?

7. When have you felt trapped by reverse discrimination, and how did you handle the situation?

Chapter 3

Seeking Acceptance

First Payment For Doubt's Benefit

There is the greatest practical benefit in making a few failures early in life.

—Thomas Henry Huxley
On Medical Education

"How much are the pumpkins?" she asked in a velvety voice. Her long skirt whipped gently in the brisk fall breeze. Her innocent face and quick smile overcame the cold eyes I still remember forty years later.

"Twenty-five cents for the big ones and fifteen cents for the small ones," I recited breathlessly, recalling what Eddie, my twelve-year-old housebrother, told those who stopped along our edge-of-town farm to buy pumpkins that October.

To my surprise, she seemed to understand the words I managed to squeeze out as the adrenalin raced through my body. I had gotten my feet to track quickly enough to go down five steps and open the front door before she had decided no one was home.

"Can I go and look at them?" she asked, smiling brightly.

"Sure," I replied, glad I could stay at the glass storm door and watch her pick out her pumpkins without going outside and stumbling behind her in an uneasy gait that is often one of the marks of cerebral palsy.

I was the only one home, but I didn't want Eddie to lose a sale just because he wasn't there. It was his project, and I didn't understand why he was not yet home from school. Pat, my housemother, usually home by the time I returned from school, was shopping, and Ted, my housefather, was still at work.

The breeze swirled golden leaves across the sidewalk as I watched the lady walk back and forth along the row of pumpkins. I remembered Eddie's cash box was on the kitchen table and quickly traced the steps in my mind I would have to take, without falling, if I would have to make change. She then came back to the house.

"I'll take those two," said the woman, as I reopened the door. She pointed to one larger pumpkin and one small pumpkin along the sidewalk.

"That'll be forty cents," I said abruptly, quickly trying to show I knew what I was doing. But, I garbled the "f" sound, stuttering so badly in the rush that what came out of my mouth sounded jumbled even to me.

"Pardon?" the woman asked briskly. Her cold, gray eyes suddenly complemented the frown on her forehead. She didn't understand.

Don't blow this, I told myself. After all, I was also twelve years old. If Eddie could sell pumpkins, I could, too. I was again short of breath.

"That'll be f-o-r-t-y cents," I repeated slowly in another choppy, breathless sentence that came out more clearly.

"Yes," she agreed. She understood and concurred. My confidence again began to bounce back from its deficit.

She opened her purse. "Do you have change?" she asked in a strangely staccato manner.

"Yes," I answered again, imagining how long it would take for me to climb up the steps to the kitchen and come back with a fistful of change. "I'll be right back," I assured her. She needn't worry. It would take time. But I would be back.

She handed me what I thought was a five-dollar bill. It felt crisp and new, as though it had never been folded before.

With the bill between my left thumb and forefinger, I climbed the five steps up to the kitchen on my hands and knees and pulled myself up to a standing position. I looked back and saw her glancing at me through the storm door.

I threw the woman's bill on the table and opened Eddie's cash box. The bills in the box, stacked neatly in a loose bundle, popped up as I opened the lid. I quickly scattered them on the table to see what he had. Lots of ones. Some fives. Some tens.

I counted out four ones, retrieved two quarters and a dime from the box and stuffed them tightly into my right fist, so I could use my left hand to paw the railing, as I descended the stairs to the front door, one step at a time.

My first sale. Eddie would be so proud, I thought, as I again reached the front door.

I opened the storm door and, instead of counting out the bills one by one, handed her the change in a wad.

"That's four dollars and sixty cents," I managed to get out in a voice that was again short of breath.

She fingered through the bills and looked puzzled. "I gave you a ten-dollar bill," she said with authority. "I need another five."

"Oh . . . I thought you gave me a five," I said with an unsure, apologetic quiver. "Let me check."

I bounced back up the steps again, asking myself how I could mistake a ten for a five. As I pulled myself up from my kneeling position at the top of the stairs, I again saw Eddie's cash scattered across the table, just as I had left it. I gathered up the fives, four in all. They were all crisp, and I couldn't recall how many there had been in the cash box.

I began to panic. You're taking too long, I told myself. She'll wonder if you're ever coming back to the front door.

I counted out three tens. Two were well worn, but one was crisp. Was that the one she had given me? It was crumpled. How could I make such a mistake?

I wished Eddie was home. He would know what to do. He would know how much cash he had on hand. I looked for a slip of paper or a note in the box to show a current total for cash on hand. Nothing.

She must be right, I told myself. I grabbed a five, scooted down the steps and threw myself off balance with my contortions upon reaching the landing. In what seemed like a fall in slow motion, I desperately reached for the storm door and caught it with my right hand knuckles just in time to avoid a bellyflop in front of the lady.

"Here's your five," I heard myself say, more aware of the temporary ache in my knuckles than the lady.

"Thank you, young man," she replied with a faint smile as she put the bill in her purse. She slung her purse over her shoulder and took the pumpkins—one by one—to her car, as I watched from the door.

I took a deep breath as she drove out of the yard—relieved, excited, and proud about making my first pumpkin sale. Though next time, I promised myself, I would pay closer attention to the business of making change.

I went back to the kitchen table, counted out the bills and change, and put the money neatly back into the box with a note, which read, "October 14, 1955: $61.75."

When Eddie returned home that evening, I eagerly told him I had sold two more of his pumpkins. But when he recounted the money in his cash box, he found himself short by five dollars.

The Hunt

My heart is a lonely hunter that hunts on a lonely hill.

—William Sharp
The Lonely Hunter

I pushed my bike up the steep driveway. It was heavier than usual. I felt sluggish.

The warm sunshine was already beginning to overpower the nippy fall air. It was the start of pheasant season, and my dad and two younger brothers, Paul and Bill, dashed here and there, getting ready for their first drive through the golden cornfields across the valley from our farmstead.

I knew I couldn't go with them, but I wasn't even asked to be a part of this annual ritual—one of the few bonding activities the men of our family enjoyed outside of the long hours of everyday chores on the farm.

I was lonely—a heavy burden that I found myself carrying on an off-and-on basis as a seventeen-year-old who had many acquaintances in school and church but no close friends.

It especially hurt when the other guys in my own family discounted me in what were the *manly* things to do during the late 1950s in rural Wisconsin.

I stopped pushing my bike, even though I was near the top of the driveway, and leaned over the seat. Big pools of tears clouded up in my eyes. I couldn't see, and I didn't care.

The bike's handlebar slipped out of my hand and suddenly rotated, throwing my limp body in one direction and the bike in another. I felt the gravel dig into my knuckles, as I tried to break my fall. I heard the bike crash.

After quickly checking the superficial cuts on my hands, I looked through my tears in each direction to see if anyone had seen what had happened. No one.

I crawled to my bike, picked it up, and once more used it for balance as I walked it over to the shade tree on our front lawn. I placed it against the trunk of the tree and sat down in the grass to nurse my wounds, feeling lucky to have avoided serious injury once again in my own private struggle with the physical dangers of my life.

It was then that I saw the new dent in the front fender of my bike. But I only gave it a passing thought. Both fenders on my bike were pocked from many falls, and yet it still worked, giving me the thrill of coasting down the hills of our farm—free and easy.

Then the time always came when the pedaling would become too difficult, and I would have to hop off and start walking it up the next hill. The free rides were not really free.

Paul and Bill were off on their free rides. They had years of hard work on the farm ahead of them. They should enjoy today's hunt.

Even at seventeen I was beginning to see that life was like that. For me, it had already become a series of ups and downs—success at tying my own shoes for the first time; backward falls which left my head bleeding and aching;

bike riding which freed me of my stiff legs; crisp, fall days when I was alone.

Somehow, though, each little setback has prompted me to go on, to do better, to fight back in ways that are constructive instead of destructive. I've found battling loneliness with indiscriminate anger is self-defeating. And the worst route to take is to give up and become a vegetable. I've had to create my own hunt through extended family relationships and professional networks for the sense of community that comes with those connections.

I consider that inner drive an innate human quality that is in all of us—that drive for being accepted, understood, appreciated, and loved. We may be lucky enough to feel that love at birth, but the volatility of everyday life both as a child and even as an adult can deplete the feeling of being loved and appreciated. Loneliness—and the need for being part of a community—is always with us.

So we search for experiences that give us a sense of community—probably based on how much positive self-regard we experienced as children.

And living with a disability makes the hunt just that much more difficult.

Necessary Expediency?

Everything comes about by way of strife and necessity.

—Heraclitus
Fragment 80

Fluffy flakes of snow drifted lazily to the pavement in the calm January morning air as she came out of her apartment building, suitcase in hand. I was anxious yet calm. I had driven up to her door at exactly 7:00 as we had arranged beforehand. That would give us forty-five minutes to get to the airport.

She opened the back door of my car and placed her suitcase in the back seat.

"Good morning," I beamed, driven by the bold risk I was taking. "Ready for the Bahamas?"

"You bet," Jennifer replied, flashing a broad, ruby-red smile. She tucked her blue raincoat around her hips as she slid into the passenger seat beside me.

She was there. I was there. Apparently, money can buy companionship, I thought.

"This is going to work?" I asked, checking one more time, before putting my car into drive.

"I'm ready to go," Jennifer confirmed. "I'm ready for some sunshine!"

"Well, then, Nassau, here we come," I said more confidently and drove out of the driveway of her apartment complex. I quickly recalled with satisfaction the imagination I mustered in proposing our arrangement for this trip.

"You got the tickets?" she asked abruptly.

I placed my left hand over the right breast pocket of my sport coat. "Yeah, they're here in my pocket," I replied, affirming our agreement.

I had met Jennifer in November after placing a classified ad in the local daily under "companionship," offering an all-expenses-paid week on New Kingston Island in exchange for helping me enjoy a carefree week away from the pressures of my public relations job and the dinginess of a drab midwestern winter.

That meant eliminating as much as possible the concerns I had as a single person with a disability in traveling alone to my time-share unit—negotiating airports, preparing simple meals, trekking to and from the beach, getting in and out of the pool.

It was an agreement based on trust, expediency, and necessity. Jennifer had written me a letter—one of several I had received—after seeing my ad. I called her, and, despite my nervous, jumbled speech, we hit it off on the phone.

At twenty-six, Jennifer was single and ready for adventure. As the recreation director for the Liberty County Nursing Home, she daily experienced the quiet, slow passage of time for the residents. She enjoyed helping them relive fond memories. In the process she found herself mentally collecting the regrets some of the residents, now feeble, felt in not pursuing their dreams while they were still able.

"Do it while we still can," I suddenly said, repeating the advice she had given me in our first telephone conversation. The snow turned to heavy, wet flakes, and I turned on the windshield wipers.

"You got it," she agreed and flipped the heater fan up one more notch.

Jennifer and I had met before Christmas for dinner at Seaman's Supper Club. A brunette with a round, dimpled face, she stood four inches taller than my five-foot-six-inch frame. She was mature, intuitive, earnest.

Jennifer had grown up with three older brothers. Her father was a truck driver. She had watched her mother patiently wait on the men in her family and promised herself that she would someday marry a man who wanted to form a more equal partnership.

At thirty-nine, I had watched my mother die a slow, mean death with cancer the year before and had promised myself more balance between an absorbing work week and a puny personal life.

I told Jennifer over the phone that I would draft a letter of agreement so we could discuss it during our dinner meeting. It spelled out what I expected and what Jennifer expected. We would each have separate bedrooms. I was not looking for a physical—or emotional—relationship.

We pulled into the airport, where the traffic was grinding the thick, white flakes into a dirty slush.

As I parked the car to unload, I could see the excitement in her brown eyes. She pursed her lips, momentarily erasing the dimples in her cheeks.

"Just think, this afternoon we'll be out of this mess and basking in the sun." Her tone was ecstatic.

Retrieving the last of our luggage from the car for the skycap, I suddenly heard, "Hi, Jim," behind me. I turned to look up at a big, graying man.

"Virgil?" I said breathlessly and shook his hand. "You flying out, too?"

"You bet. Florida," Virgil chuckled. The large snowflakes were accumulating on his black wool coat.

"Virgil, this is Jennifer," I managed to say. "Jennifer, this is Virgil Mann. Virgil and I went to Africa together. He just retired as state secretary of agriculture."

"Hi, Virgil. I'm Jim's traveling companion for this trip," Jennifer replied. "We're going to Nassau."

"That's great," Virgil said, turning away. "You both have a nice time. Got to check in."

"We do, too," I jumped in. "Have a good trip. Jennifer, you can take the tickets. I'll park the car and meet you at the ticket counter."

I parked the car and walked through the parking lot alone with my clanking crutches. Each step echoed off the concrete above me and reinforced my uneasiness. "Traveling companion," I repeated to myself. It sounded so utilitarian when Jennifer actually used those words to describe her role to Virgil.

Did he interpret that to mean "personal caregiver"? Was I shortchanging myself, pretending to be satisfied with a one-dimensional relationship with Jennifer? Were we about to reinforce the stereotype many people still have about a person with a physical disability: that I shouldn't expect a single female to be attracted to me as a person?

Was Jennifer compromising herself by being *paid* to do for me what she grudgingly did for her brothers and father while she was living at home?

I came out of the parking garage and skidded my crutches gingerly across the street to the check-in entry door. When I finally reached the door, cold flakes of snow had begun to accumulate on my eyebrows and melt over my glasses. I needed the warmth and sunshine of the Bahamas.

The Neighbor I Never Met

Through our own recovered innocence we discern the innocence of our neighbors.

—Henry David Thoreau
Walden

The doorbell rang. It was a clear, fresh sound that mingled with the smell of carpet glue in our new home and sent shots of joy and pride through my veins.

"I'll get it," Pam announced from the hallway. I heard her open the front door to our first visitor. I jumped up from my desk in the den and grabbed a serving cart on casters that I had found handy in helping me navigate the wide, open spaces of our new house without the usual awkwardness of crutches.

The solid oak cart moved stiffly across the new carpet. The top of the cart was top-heavy with the day's mail and newspapers, and I wasn't moving fast enough to meet Pam at the front door.

"Pam, I'm coming!" I shouted in a slurred rush, hoping I wasn't missing something exciting we could be sharing together. I reached the hallway and saw a small woman under the light of our entryway. Pam held a paper plate wrapped in foil.

"Hi, I'm Jim," I announced. I heard it plainly and pleasantly in my brain, but it came out hurriedly and distorted. The woman quickly receded down the steps before I could get to the door.

"Thank you very much," Pam called after her, and the woman disappeared into the darkness.

"Who was that?" I asked, out of breath as I finally got to the door.

"One of our neighbors. She gave us some brownies as a housewarming gift."

"Nice. What's her name?"

"I don't know." Pam looked puzzled. "She just said 'I'm your neighbor' and that she had baked us some brownies. I was just about to ask her and then you came and she suddenly left."

"That's odd," I reflected. "Why wouldn't she stay a minute so we could get to know each other a little bit?"

"I think she saw you coming," Pam said in a matter-of-fact tone that did not hide her disgust or disappointment.

"I just wanted to introduce myself," I murmured, giving myself an alibi. But I knew what Pam meant.

And perhaps I knew what our neighbor had just experienced. It's easier to avoid what could be a potentially unpleasant situation than have to face it and deal with the consequences.

I remember settling for an obstructed view of the basketball court on the end of the high school gym's bleachers instead of walking stiffly in front of the crowd and drawing attention to myself just to get a better seat. I recall hugging the wall near established acquaintances at an after-work cocktail party instead of mingling with the group and meeting new people. I admit asking a colleague to present my ideas to a group of second-level managers instead of doing it myself.

Being human, after all, is continually fighting the habit of flight from what we don't expect and what could be unpleasant.

But, deep within ourselves, we know our souls soon begin to shrivel, if we slip haphazardly into only satisfying our need for comfortableness. Comfort without challenge lulls us into complacency. We can become hollow shells—neurotic, self-centered, and old.

"She wasn't comfortable with your disability," Pam said as she went into the kitchen.

"I don't think we can say that," I countered, following her with the cart in front of me to our kitchen island. "She brought the brownies, after all. She must have seen us together before—working in the yard, shopping downtown . . . "

I uncovered the paper plate and snatched one of the thick, brown squares.

"She was uncomfortable," Pam stoically repeated. "She saw you coming and took off."

"Maybe she was just shy," I said softly. "Maybe she just didn't know how to go about meeting us."

"Maybe," Pam allowed, as she also helped herself to a brownie. "People tend to go by what they see."

We never saw our neighbor-who-brought-the-brownies again.

Out But Not Yet In

Include me out.

—Samuel Goldwyn

"More handicapped people are coming out," I heard Jack whisper across the table to Tom, nodding slightly in my direction. Jack, one of twenty-four people in management who had gathered for our workshop about how to manage change effectively, was sitting three feet from me on my side of the table.

Tom, sitting kitty-cornered from me, realized I was eavesdropping in amusement. He had a smirk on his face but said nothing. His eyes met mine for a second but then flashed back to Jack.

"And women," Jack continued, wide-eyed, still not speaking to me. "I took another management workshop a couple of months ago, and almost a third of the class were women."

"I can believe that," Tom agreed, still wearing a whimsical look.

Jack was conveniently ignoring me, even though I had introduced myself to both of my table partners after parking my crutches and grabbing a chair. I had ventured outside my daily routine of familiar contacts and encountered another reaction to my disability from a person I hadn't met before.

Knowing that my gestures and facial expressions often appear distorted and exaggerated to strangers, I tried to shape a slight grin on my face to let Tom know I wasn't offended. In fact, I felt privileged to have my own private view of human nature. It was like leaving my fly open and documenting, in my mind, the people who would draw my attention to my unfortunate oversight.

It was 1985, and, yes, I had come out. In fact, I had been out a long time. Jack didn't know that I had been taking workshops and courses every spring and fall since I had graduated from college in 1965.

But he was probably right. I was unusual and incongruous. I was in management; I had a disability. Yet, the fact I was vice president of communication for Heartland Dairies didn't seem to surprise him. Perhaps he didn't understand me when I introduced myself.

It was five years before the Americans with Disabilities Act, and apparently more of us with disabilities were coming out all the time. I just didn't see them in the circles I frequented. And, apparently, Jack hadn't either. That was not surprising because I considered just being "out" an accomplishment—something many others with a disability had not yet achieved.

More than twenty years earlier, I remember receiving little guidance from the School of Journalism's placement office at the University of Wisconsin-Madison, mostly because I was probably the first journalism student with a severe disability to earn a degree.

"We believe you'll be able to work on a job," Professor Abernathy, my advisor, told me a couple of weeks before graduation, as he stroked his black, narrow tie.

In one sense, that was reassuring. He was a former advertising executive who had blandly settled into academic life and written several stiff textbooks about advertising, promotion, and public relations. He had, at least, been in the job market.

On the other hand, I could see he was going against the prevalent philosophy on campus at the time. After all, a university education was to help me learn how to learn so I could live life to the fullest. The vocational benefits were only secondary. Professor Abernathy knew, however, my priorities were more utilitarian than that; I needed to get a job. I needed to support myself.

At the same time, I felt uncomfortable. He was telling me something I already knew in my heart—something so basic that I almost started to laugh when he said it, thinking he was trying a bit of wry humor on me.

Yes, I could probably hold a job. Professor Abernathy was serious when he said it, and I saw the uneasiness in his eyes behind his rimless glasses. I thanked him, after realizing he had no advice about what careers in journalism held the most promise and how well my temperament and skills matched the requirements of those jobs.

I was headed for a safety net—a soft landing out of the mainstream of business. Dr. Reichman, a professor who specialized in the community press, recommended I take a state civil service exam so I could qualify for an editing job with a state government agency.

But I didn't want to get lost forever in the stifling state bureaucracy or in sheltered employment that shielded me from the real world. So I chose instead to prove myself with a typewriter and camera, translating what I observed and heard in the dairy plants and cow barns of Wisconsin into a coherent magazine for Heartland's members.

More than twenty years later, I still found it exciting to return to the university campus on a routine basis to talk about about management theory and then grapple with the challenge of how I could transfer those ideas into practical programs that would work in rural Wisconsin.

Dr. Stewart, our workshop instructor for the day, finally stepped in front of our group, and the six tables of participants quieted.

"We're going to begin today by first experiencing what it's like to manage change," Dr. Stewart began. "I'd like you to count off by ones and twos, starting with Jack, here."

The toes in my left shoe curled. Another icebreaker. I dreaded icebreakers because I didn't have agility or the speaking ability to pull them off with aplomb. In fact, they just emphasized my disability.

"You, Jim, can sit this one out and observe because this could get quite physical," he said quickly, pointing to me. I watched as the others started to count. One. Two. One. Two. One. Two . . . I soon found myself at a table by myself, relieved but still conspicuous.

"Those of you who are ones are going to be blindfolded," Dr. Stewart continued quickly. "The twos are your guides and helpers . . . "

I was out but still not in, included but still apart.

Difficult Terrain

First keep the peace within yourself,
then you can also bring peace to others.

—Thomas a Kempis
The Imitation of Christ

He had never let me down. Even when the going got tough, he had never dropped me.

It is real to this day. I hear him grunt under my weight. With my frail body wrapped around his beefy back—my feet dangling as he clutches my knees and holds them firmly against his waist—I grab at his surprisingly small shoulders, locking my thin arms around his neck. I dig my chin into the back of his neck, trusting he will not fall.

Paul is three years younger than I, yet at ten he can haul me on his back along the dusty cowpaths and across the rippling creek in our Back Forty.

I can feel his disproportionately small feet search tentatively for the next step in the dirt path, avoiding half-exposed rocks and sun-baked cow pies. We are both just the right size so piggyback riding works.

We knew and understood each other's needs back then in a simplistic way that we lost over the years and now, thirty-seven years later, would never regain.

Still, we probably didn't really know each other at all—not as high schoolers, college students, or mature adults—even though Paul instinctively knew when I needed a supporting hand to keep my balance or a relevant comment to help a stranger understand my garbled speech.

"I'm going to walk up the ravine a little way," Pam announced, breaking my thoughts. Her voice sounded startlingly close as she suddenly appeared out of a thicket down by the gurgling stream.

"Look what I found," Pam said slowly, almost to herself, as she came up the knoll. She was using a gnarled but sturdy piece of a thick tree branch, long stripped of its leaves and twigs, as a walking stick. "Just the right size."

"I'll stay here," I answered in a stupor, hearing her but responding to her first comment. The early fall sun was warm but not too hot. The gentle breeze brought a fresh tinge to the pungent scent of mature foliage expecting the first frost, but the smell of cedar hung close to me and overpowered every other aroma.

I sat on the cedar bench and admired the handiwork of Scott, Paul's son, and Glenn, his son-in-law. My feet barely hit the cement beneath the bench. A little too high, maybe, I thought. And a little shallow in the seat.

A bit of sawdust, patches of bare earth, and nuggets of excess cement made the bench stand out from the thicket behind it but not as much as the sloping rectangle of clipped grass that ran down to the stream and to a tree-line view of the sun in the west. The fallen tree to the south blocked the old cowpath down the steep side hill leading to the site.

Spectacular view but sequestered. It was the spot Paul had chosen. And—his style.

The sun was making me drowsy, so I lay full length on the narrow bench, looking up at the leaves against the blue, hazy sky above me, knowing he was close by. Just two months before, his wife, Cindy, had sprinkled his ashes in criss-cross fashion up and down the hillside clearing as the family watched along the stream below.

Dead at forty-seven. I repeated the four words to myself, as if that would have made them more real. He had fought the brain tumor for twelve months, but toward the end he was frail and even started to walk like I do—in an unsteady gait and shuffle that betrayed his pretense of balance.

And now I was lying there with him in his resting place of peace. I closed my eyes.

Paul turned out to be a quiet man, essentially known only by his immediate family and a few close friends. He and I could have talked about the things we began to have in common, once he had cancer. The step-by-step uncertainty of trying to walk into the next room. The attention he received every time he appeared in public. The necessity of letting people know he had a clear mind. The need to get things done. The sadness. The anger. The fear. The resignation. The suicide. Death.

No. That would have been too much to expect. We could have talked for hours. We should have. But we didn't. The sibling rivalry, the tension between first and second son, the increased attention I received as a child from family and friends because of my disability—each drove wedges between us that we never tried to remove. Pam had recognized the problem years before. She was right, but I hadn't done anything about it.

And Paul, in facing death, had gone far beyond where I was in his spiritual journey through life. Was it my place to intrude by trying to break down barriers that took years to build?

I accepted but didn't understand. I was disappointed yet, at the same time, filled with admiration for him. I felt guilty and complacent.

"Jim!" Jim!" I heard Pam's urgent call—this time more distant but still close enough to reach me easily where I was resting.

I tried to sit up but instead rolled off the narrow bench with a thump onto the loose earth below, turning my body downhill to break the impact of the fall. I jarred my ribs with my own elbow.

"What do you want?" I called out angrily—deriding myself for missed opportunities, disturbed at my lack of discernment, upset by Pam's call, concerned about my ribs. I scrambled to pick myself up. In the process, I realized I wasn't hurt.

"There you are," Pam said, suddenly appearing from the thicket above me. She sounded pleased and surprised.

"Why did you call?" I growled in fractured vowels.

"I thought I was lost. What happened?"

"I thought you were in trouble, and then I fell off the bench," I said more calmly, needing sympathy.

"You all right?"

"Yeah." There was no need to go into details about Paul. We had covered that many times before.

"You know, a walking stick is a good idea—especially in the woods like this," Pam was saying as I gathered my crutches. "I'm going to keep it."

We ducked under the fallen tree and proceeded up the cowpath—I with my Canadian crutches, Pam with her walking stick.

"You feel bad?" Pam asked again, recognizing my melancholy about Paul's death. We were approaching the steepest part of the hill leading back to our car.

"I'm OK."

The hill seemed steeper and more difficult going up than it had been coming down. We automatically switched to our tandem mode for difficult terrain: I held her slender shoulder with my left hand for more substantial support while she used my left crutch. But this was a little different. She poked the walking stick, in her right hand, ahead of us and gradually pulled us, in tandem, up the hill.

How Does Seeking Acceptance Apply to Your Situation?

1. How have you learned to avoid deferring to the judgment of others when you needed to trust your own instincts?

2. Under what circumstances have you successfully fulfilled your need for friendship and community when traditional means were not working?

3. In what cases have you learned not to compromise your dreams by settling for the second-best alternative just because you were different?

4. How have you learned to understand the feelings of others who hesitate to associate with you because you are different?

5. How have you bridged the gap between being "out" and being "in"?

6. How have you come to terms with the disappointment of missed opportunities for friendship and community?

Chapter 4

Developing Composure

Just Along For the Ride

Women try their luck; men risk theirs.

—Oscar Wilde
The Picture of Dorian Gray

"Wouldn't you rather have a Buick?" Lisa sang out as her blonde hair whipped in the wind from the open car windows. She gave a throaty laugh and downshifted her new '78 Regal as we approached a herd of Holsteins crossing the gravel road.

Yes, I was with a blonde in a new Buick. My dream of being with a sharp girl who understood me was coming true. My spirit soared in the spring air.

But, at the same time, something about Lisa troubled me. Perhaps she was too flippant, too carefree. Was she really interested in me? Or was I just along for the ride?

The grumble of the idling V-8, the racket of the herd and the sharp barks of the cow dog echoed off the shadowy Kickapoo hills on both sides of us. The cows pushed against each other to get away from the dog and down into the pasture below. The sun had just dipped below the jagged horizon of oak and maple, creating a stark silhouette against a western sky of orange and blue hues.

In blue-and-white-striped bib overalls, the farmer followed the dog that snipped at the dirty tails of the last cows to cross the gravel. As the cows disappeared, the soft chatter of the frogs and crickets from the creek below filled the calm twilight air.

We both waved at the farmer, who raised his walking stick in reply. Lisa inched our way across the new path of fresh cow manure so it wouldn't splatter her royal blue car.

We then scurried up the winding gravel road out of the fresh scent of cow manure, which temporarily overpowered the new-car smell. Once we reached the top of the ridge, the manure smell gradually left us. The last rays from the setting sun behind us cast a faint but distorted shadow of the Regal along my side of the road's ditch.

"We should be able to get WLS up here," Lisa said hopefully and leaned over to tune in the Midwest's most powerful rock station from Chicago. "Come on, 50,000 watts of power!"

The four-speaker Delco stereo radio produced only a faint static with a few blips here and there as Lisa cranked the tuning knob toward 90. Then she hit it. "A little luck . . . a little, little, little luck . . . "

I could feel the cluck of the harmony, so mellow, bounce off the white, perforated ceiling of the Regal and escape through the windows as we softly cruised away from the sunset. Across the broad horizon, the cloudless sky was turning orange, then blue-gray, and then purple as we headed east.

Lisa beamed as she started snapping the fingers of her right hand to the beat. We looked at each other. Her eyes were full of delight. She giggled and started harmonizing with the duet. "A little luck . . . a little luck . . . a little, little, little luck . . . "

It was another one of our "after-work dates." Lisa and I worked in the same office, where I had left my car in the parking lot so we could try out her new car.

She was a marketing manager, and I was communication director. Both raised on dairy farms, we were the first generation in both of our families to get off-the-farm jobs. She was barely thirty; I was thirty-five. We had each worked for more than ten years for the local dairy cooperative which manufactured the milk from its member farmers into butter and cheese.

We both knew life was fragile. Lisa's sister had died from leukemia in 1963. Her father had died from a brain tumor in 1976. She understood what my family had gone through during my mother's twenty-four-year battle with cancer.

And she understood what it was like to have career aspirations as a woman in a workplace dominated by men where women were governed by different rules.

Maybe all of these circumstances helped her to overlook my physical disabilities. Being with a guy who had cerebral palsy didn't seem to make much difference to her.

But riding with a blonde in a blue Buick into that quiet May night came close to fulfilling one of my fantasies. With a little luck our relationship could develop into something good for us both.

The road flattened and turned into blacktop. Lisa pumped the car up to sixty. The darkening sky arched the ridge and valleys to the north and south. This was Lisa's home country. She had grown up on the next ridge.

"Let's stop and see Joe," she said with a sparkle in her eyes. "You remember Joe. He came to our delegate meeting last year."

"Tall guy with a crew cut?" I said stiffly, not at all liking the idea of stopping at another guy's place.

"Yeah," She replied with a raised eyebrow and quick smile. "Joe has really helped us a lot since Dad died."

"That's good," I agreed, wondering how often they had gotten together.

"He and John have taken over the farm from their folks," she said. "They retired last fall, you know."

We drove into Joe's U-shaped driveway, which linked a white house, trimmed lawn, and a hundred-foot red barn. The lights in both the house and barn were on. With a familiarity that surprised me, Lisa drove up to the barn door and tooted her horn.

Joe stuck his head around the corner of the open barn door and stood, silhouetted, against the two rows of bright lights in the empty stanchion barn. He then moved with deliberate steps toward us, as if unsure who was sitting in the dark, silent car. Wearing a white T-shirt and blue jeans, he bent down to look into Lisa's window.

"Wouldn't you rather have a Buick?" Lisa gushed.

"When'd ya get this!?" Joe, a pleasant-looking man with a broad forehead and blonde crewcut, asked with a chuckle.

"Tuesday," Lisa replied.

"How many miles did'ya have on your other one?" Joe inquired.

"Ninety thousand," Lisa said. "They count up fast. Joe, you know Jim Hasse, communication director at the Dairies?"

"Oh, sure," he replied after quickly eyeing my crutches in the back seat.

"You have a nice place here," I said, trying to be polite but not necessarily putting my best effort into making my garbled speech understandable. "How many cows are you milking?"

"How many cows are you milking?" Lisa repeated after a pause, realizing Joe didn't understand me.

"About ninety," Joe said, directing his reply more to Lisa than to me.

"You've been at that level for a while," Lisa commented.

"Well, yeah, since Mom and Dad retired. And when John got out of high school, we decided to beef the herd up a bit, too."

"That's a lot of work," I said more plainly.

"Yeah, but there's two of us and Dad still helps out now and then," Joe replied, this time speaking directly to me. "We just finished chores. Wanna come in the house?"

"No," Lisa declined. "We've gotta get back."

"You doing anything Saturday night?" Joe asked Lisa in a lower voice, as if I couldn't hear or didn't count. I gulped and felt myself sinking into the passenger seat. In my mind I pretended not to be next to a blonde in a blue Buick. But Joe was still there, his burly arms folded against his chest.

"I don't know yet," Lisa replied, almost inaudibly in the still night air. She started the car and turned on the headlights. "Call me Thursday."

Beyond Boundaries

I can endure my own despair, but not another's hope.

—William Walsh, song

I placed my suitcase on the queen bed. The darkened bedroom was musty with the sea air I had come to associate with my week of vacation in the Bahamas. Thin bands of midday sun from the closed blinds hit the bedspread of orange, green, and beige. It was a quiet, warm, and inviting room. But it was empty. I had to get out.

I shuffled toward the hallway without my crutches and grabbed at the wall for balance. I suddenly found myself sobbing uncontrollably—and shocked at my lack of composure.

Jennifer, already in her swimsuit and thongs, came out of the bathroom.

"Carol should be here—Carol should be here," I unintelligibly repeated between deep sobs, revealing in one outburst the rage and the hurt I had buried during the previous two months.

Shame then enveloped my grief as I realized I was revealing what I had promised myself I would not tell Jennifer. All she needed to know I had already told her. I had someone cancel out on me for this year's week at my timeshare unit in the Bahamas. She was free that week in February and had again agreed to be my traveling companion, as she had last year, to Nassau.

Jennifer handed me some tissue from the bathroom. Her wide, blue eyes met mine, and through my tears I could see both concern and disgust. "Are you all right?" Her tone revealed more of a sense of duty than empathy.

"Yeah," I said in one grunt. I massaged the tissue into a wad and used it to blot my eyes, which were beginning to sting from my avalanche of tears. I knew it was what she wanted to hear. We were here to have fun and forget.

Through the patio door at the opposite end of the hallway, I could see the sun glimmer across the blue water of the pool just outside the two-bedroom bungalow.

We went out onto the patio where we each sank into a deck chair—I in my traveling clothes and Jennifer in her bathing suit.

My eyes were puffy and burning. Without looking, I reached into my shirt pocket for my sunglasses, put them on and lay back in the deck chair. Despite the warm sun, a shiver ran down my spine, and a deep sigh involuntarily shuddered through my chest, releasing the tension I didn't know I had about this trip. I needed some rest. I needed a break from my daily rat race at work. I needed to forget about Carol.

In my mind, I saw Carol and me and her two boys before the warm fireplace late Christmas Eve, telling funny stories and trying to muffle our squeals of merriment for fear we would wake up Carol's parents in their bedroom on the second floor above us. At that moment, we were a family.

It had been an unusually warm Christmas in 1982, even

for Tennessee. Yet, at that time, we were both looking forward to "our" week in the Bahamian sun.

But after the holidays and the return to work, Carol became irritated at the most mundane things—squeaky windshield wipers, my noisy crutches, stale chewing gum, my mumbled speech. The problem finally came out. I was a good man, Carol allowed, but I lacked what she called *passion*, both physically and mentally—a thirst for getting what one is due in life.

She couldn't picture herself going through life with a man who walked so slowly with crutches, and she needed to go back home with her family to be closer to her parents and siblings in Tennessee.

"You'll never find someone else like me." Carol's words ran over and over in my head as I felt the sun penetrate my forehead and arms.

I looked over at Jennifer. Her eyes closed, she was propping her face up at an angle to take full advantage of the late-afternoon sun. Without opening her eyes, she adjusted the straps of her one-piece, blue bathing suit. Her thin lips, still wearing a hint of ruby-red lipstick, smiled with contentment but not enough to dimple her cheeks.

I first met her two years before when she had answered my "personals" classified ad for an all-expenses-paid traveling companion.

Relaxed, feeling some closure, and again looking forward to my week of vacation, I faced the sun and dozed off until I heard Jennifer call from the patio door.

"Want something to drink?" she asked, as if she were the resident waitress.

"No, thanks," I replied in a groggy haze. I looked up and watched her put on a floral sun dress over her bathing suit. Continually on a diet, Jennifer was about five feet, ten inches tall and carried her weight well.

"I'm going down to check out the beach," she said as she went through the patio gate.

Rolling over onto my left side, I felt the sun hit my back and again fell asleep.

I woke up in a shadow and brisk breeze. Inside the bungalow, I didn't find Jennifer. Slipping on my Canadian crutches, I left the bungalow and negotiated across the narrow boardwalk which spanned a gully on the way to the beach. By the time I reached the sand, a stiff breeze was churning the waves into hefty whitecaps. There was no one on the beach.

A government helicopter, new to the island in just the last two years, flew down the beach from north to south, patrolling the shore for drug traffic.

I returned to the bungalow, closed the patio doors to keep out the cool breeze, turned on the lights, and had a salami sandwich, orange, and Coke. This never happened last year. Jennifer and I pretty much stuck together—going out to eat at night, visiting the straw market, lying on the beach.

I settled down on the green and beige sofa to re-read, in uneasy spurts, Salinger's *Catcher in the Rye.* Somehow, at thirty-seven, I better understood what Salinger was trying to say than when I had first read his book at seventeen and was hung up on four-letter words.

By 8:30, it was almost dark, and I became truly concerned about Jennifer. She had been gone about five hours. But I decided to wait.

By 10:30, I was tired and ready for bed but couldn't sleep—torn by fantasies about what had happened to Jennifer. Scooped up by a tidal wave. Snatched by drug dealers. Raped by another tourist.

At midnight, I woke up in a start. Jennifer was still not back. I called the security people for our compound.

"Is your wife?" one of the guards asked in broken English when they came to the bungalow to investigate.

"No," I answered slowly. "She's my traveling companion."

He either didn't understand my garbled speech or the jargon of the personal ads in the States. He probably had problems with both. Anyway, they searched the beach and found nothing.

At 2:00, there was another knock at the door. It was Jennifer, wet and windblown. "I forgot my key," she apologized. Then she brightened.

"We just came from the beach," she said, trying to hide a smile. "This is Tony." She pulled a slim, young Bahamian from the dark, and they both came into the bungalow. "He's going to sleep here tonight. Tony, this is Jim."

I shook Tony's hand but immediately blasted Jennifer. "Where have you been? I was so worried I had security out looking for you!"

"Jim," Jennifer answered more calmly, "I'm an adult!"

I went to my bedroom and slammed the door, ashamed, humiliated, and yet relieved that she was all right.

At 7:00, I woke up with a headache. The sun was out, but I dreaded leaving my bedroom and dozed off again. At 9:00, I was ready for the patio. As I walked through the hallway to the kitchen, I passed the second bedroom. Through the open door, I saw Jennifer and Tony, still asleep, sprawled on the bed together.

Drawing Out Each Other's Delusions

I dwell in Possibility—
A fairer House than Prose—
More numerous of Windows—
Superior—for Doors.

—Emily Dickinson

I know how it must feel to be healed—almost. It was 1975 (before the 1980s brought us Jimmy Bakker, freeway shootings, and street people).

I was walking back to my car with the routine clank-clank of my worn Canadian crutches marking each step when he came, in a long overcoat, stumbling out of the Square Tavern.

He moved so fast (or I moved so slowly) he caught me right at the parking meter before I could reach my car door.

"Could I touch you?" he slurred, almost in a command.

Before I could reply, he placed his right forefinger firmly on my forehead. I then had a chance to look into his face. His eyes, deep-set, raced from side to side. His mouth skewed to the right.

With my forehead tipped at a 45-degree angle, I still managed to glance down the street to see if anyone was watching. It was empty. I was more embarrassed than frightened, and scenes of evangelist Oral Roberts healing people on TV flashed before my eyes. Was this another put-on?

I chuckled to myself, expecting him to release the pressure on my forehead and be on his way.

But he didn't. He pressed his finger even more firmly on my brow to the point where I had to readjust my grip on my crutches to keep my balance.

I always had these youthful delusions of how much my crutches would come in handy if I were ever attacked. I'd whip and punish anyone who would come near me with the leverage I had in my crutches and the power I had in my arms.

Instead, I just stood there in this unnatural configuration with a stranger forcing his finger into what I'm sure had become a scowl. Yet I didn't feel I was in any danger.

Suddenly, his finger left me.

"I hope it helps you," he said with a confidence that surprised me just as much as the forcefulness of his finger.

"Thank you," I mumbled, still struck by his conviction. I was grateful to be free, careful not to disturb, respectful of his delusion.

He left, sweeping down the street, and, as I threw my crutches into the back seat of my car and slid under the wheel, I chastised myself for being such an easy touch.

I also felt relieved, amused, and energized.

It was like going through the dread of a physical and the anticipation of pain beforehand and then realizing it was over with everything checking out OK.

How many people are in a position to have something like this happen to them? Perhaps many. Maybe a few. In any case, perhaps we're each put on this earth to draw out each other's delusions—and learn.

I then found myself flexing my limbs. Were they different? Were they just a little bit more nimble, more manageable? Would a lifelong dream of healing come true? No.

As I drove down the street, I decided to give the guy a few more days to work his wonders.

Pretense

Be a fox to recognize traps
and a lion to frighten wolves.

—Niccolo Machiavelli
The Prince

Amid two thousand people in the Grande Ballroom, I felt cramped for space and alone in spirit.

"Do you want a key?" I heard Charlie across the table from me ask his companion. He was balding, probably thirty-five, and had a cockiness about him that didn't disguise past heartaches. Perhaps a recent divorce, I thought. Sheila was also past her prime but gushed at nearly everything her roommate said.

"No-o-o, honey. That's OK," Sheila assured him with a quiet giggle. "I'll pack tonight."

As I sat there at a table of ten strangers for our noon luncheon, I wondered how many single rooms, officially occupied, went unused at the Grande Hotel in Toronto during the four-day conference of the International Association of Business Communicators. Everyone was silent. I chuckled to myself—discovering, in the process, how heavy my chest felt.

"Do you use an outside design firm for your publication?" I asked Charlie, trying to make my garbled speech understandable. Someone had to start a general conversation.

"Yeah, we farm it out," he replied. " . . . Best way." It turned out he edited an employee publication in Phoenix.

"You have a designer?" he asked Sheila.

"No way," she again replied with a slight but annoying giggle. "I'm a one-person shop."

Finally, our first course came—a chilled but hotly spiced soup that no one at our table seemed to relish. It dampened the already sparse conversation.

I pulled back into my shell. I heard people nearby break out in laughter and glanced over at Sue, sitting at the third table to my left, and watched her animated gestures bring another round of softer giggles. I wished she were there beside me to add sparkle to this group. But after last night—maybe not.

It was 1978, and the first rumblings of the women's movement were just now being felt in rural Wisconsin and in the cooperative movement.

I had hired Sue as public relations coordinator after she had spent six years working her way up from a secretary to communication coordinator in a state banking association.

She was the first woman who did not have a secretarial or clerical position within our company, which had five hundred employees.

Sue was as eager to apply her developing skills in public relations and volunteer management as I was in proving to our new general manager that I could effectively manage a growing function within our organization.

She had broken out of the secretarial ranks at a time when the glass ceiling was as yet unknown because very few women had risen high enough in corporate America to touch it. Her immediate challenge was to become accepted as a professional in a corporate culture that didn't recognize females beyond the secretarial and clerical level.

As one of the few college graduates in the organization and a successful tactical person with eleven years experience as a writer and photographer, I faced the challenge of making the jump into program and people management—and overcoming the perception that someone who had difficulty walking and talking could not effectively lead.

Sue and I were beginning to learn the tough lessons of business—adjusting to the changing battle lines each workday seemed to bring. How to establish an executive-secretary relationship. How to challenge and inspire a group of sales people without appearing to be too aggressive. How to gain influence with top management. How to break out of the shell of paternalism.

We were learning that some of our visible victories only served to reinforce the stereotypes we were trying to change.

I encouraged Sue to attend the Toronto conference because I thought it would be a learning experience for her. After some hesitation, our general manager approved my request—not so that both Sue and I would grow professionally and benefit the company but because he thought I would need help in negotiating the airports in Milwaukee and Toronto.

Then, of course, there were the winks and little grins from the other male staff members and snide remarks about sharing a hotel room. In one sense, I understood their teasing because Sue was the first woman in the organization to attend an international conference. But I also loathed their insinuations and was embarrassed for them.

Sue and I each had deeper struggles, too, that motivated us but never surfaced in our conversations. Married and a mother at nineteen, Sue had outgrown her marriage during the last ten years and probably saw no way out except through financal independence. I dreamed of creating a personal life for myself (which, at this point, I lacked), gaining some sense of financial security and having a home, marriage, family.

Under the dimmed chandeliers of the Grande Hotel ballroom, I picked at my asparagus spears.

"First time in Toronto?" I asked Jill, a woman in her late twenties, who sat quietly next to me at our table.

"Yeah, I'm from St. Louis," Jill replied. "It feels so European here."

"I know what you mean," I said. "I'm from Wisconsin."

"Have you taken the subway, yet?" Jill asked.

"Yeah, last night. It's just great," I replied. "So clean."

That was not entirely true. Sue and I had gone down to the subway platform and watched the trains stop and start. The doors opened and closed so fast—just like I had seen in New York and Moscow. In both cases, it had taken two people—one on each side of me—to scoot me in and out of the cars because my feet wouldn't track fast enough to keep up with the crowd and the doors.

Sue and I had been tempted to get on the train and ride to the next stop for some shopping and dinner at Stacey's, a well-known restaurant in town, but I hesitated, deciding to play it safe.

Instead, we did the shops on Hyde Street next to the hotel and took a taxi for seafood at Hennesy's, a tugboat-turned-eatery in the harbor. During our taxi ride back to the hotel, I chided myself for not being venturesome enough to try the subway and see more of Toronto.

We got back to the fourteenth floor of our hotel. We both had rooms at the end of the long hallway—large rooms with high ceilings and panoramic views of the city.

"You've got to see my room," coaxed Sue. "I can see the harbor from my window."

It was beautiful, and we stood there, chattering about this and that light from the ships in the harbor.

"I've got to go," I said at last, beginning to feel uneasy.

"Want to see my breasts?" she asked in the same confident tone she had used in pointing out the lights in the harbor.

I was shocked—eager—glad—afraid—guarded—prepared—professional.

I ignored her question, pretending to not have heard it, and went back to my room—absorbed by her fantasy, disappointed in my naiveté.

Go to Plan 'B'

There is a moment of difficulty and danger at which flattery and falsehood can no longer deceive, and simplicity itself can no longer be misled.

—Laure Junot Abrantes
Letters of Junius

All of a sudden I had chocolate milk all over my face. It shot right into my bifocals and started dripping down my shirt into my lap.

I could feel it in my nostrils and went into a brief panic. I was drowning. I tried to take a breath and, instead, let out a long, loud snort.

I took off my glasses and grabbed some paper toweling to wipe off my red face, blue shirt, crimson tie, and navy suit pants.

"I'm sorry," I said softly, trying to express my regret that such a stupid thing should happen during an executive staff meeting in which we were trying to finalize our contingency plans for the upcoming year.

"That's OK," the president replied for the whole group of six other vice presidents. We sat around a rectangular conference table, eating our high-cholesterol lunches of cold French fries, tough Reuben sandwiches, and milk.

The vice president of finance announced, "I'll get some more paper toweling." He left the room on the run.

But that didn't relieve the tension. No one else spoke for a moment.

"Damn suit," I finally said. "I just got it dry cleaned."

Several of the guys chuckled. It was not that what I said was so funny. I glanced around the table and detected tinges of discomfort—mixed with some pity and a realization that such an incident could happen to each of them.

I could see each of them questioning themselves about how they would react, if they had received the milk bath.

"How you going to explain that one to Pam?" the vice president of manufacturing finally chided. "Coming home with chocolate milk all over yourself?"

"I'll do my Superman switch before I walk in the front door," I shot back, and we all laughed.

"You can go clean up if you want," the president said. We'll go on with our meeting."

"No, that's OK," I declined. "Not much you can do with chocolate stains."

"How about dropping your suit off at the dry cleaners on the way home?" one of the other guys suggested. "Pam won't think a thing of it if you walk in the door in your underwear."

"I'll take my chances with a stained suit," I replied.

Another chuckle.

As we went on with our meeting, I privately cussed those pint milk cartons and vowed always to bring a solid coffee mug to our monthly staff meetings so I could drink my milk from a cup.

For the first forty-eight years of my life I had gotten by. I thought I had mastered America's masculine way of drinking milk from a carton without a straw. I'd carefully grab the carton with both hands, steady it on the table, tip it slightly and bring my head down to drink from the v-shaped spout.

BREAK OUT

I can usually judge how firm my grip will be around something crushable such as a milk carton.

But I was edgy that day—and daring. I sat straight in my chair and raised the carton to my mouth while it was still full of milk. Suddenly, an involuntary squeeze from both of my hands collapsed the cardboard carton, forcing the milk into my face like a syringe.

Milk in a carton was one more item to add to my internal list of "What To Do Ifs," a mix of merely embarrassing situations as well as the truly dangerous that I have learned to anticipate, diffuse, or avoid through the years.

A Bent Fork

Conform and be dull.

—J. Frank Dobie
The Voice of the Coyote

I didn't appreciate its significance at the time. I thought it was hokey, so I threw it into the dump one day with yellowed notebooks, old *Time* magazines and broken pencils, as I cleaned my home office in a fit of tidiness. It was old, crude, and falling apart—a relic of the past. But now I wish I had kept it.

It was a four-by-eight wooden plaque which had been on my office wall at Heartland Dairies for thirteen years. A cheap dinner fork, flattened at the tip of the handle and attached to the plaque by a single rivet, rested horizontally across the piece of wood without a pin for its tine end.

The handle, on the other hand, was bent into a bow-like configuration and abruptly popped out of the plaque. Below the fork a golden rectangular plate, glued crookedly onto the wood, read, "Dunn's Supper Club, Clayton, Wis, October, 1981."

Eight of us sat around the table that night, emotionally drained from long days of preparation but excited about the merger plans we were going to present to the employees and members of the Clayton plant the next day.

I had ordered steak and immediately began to carve the meat into small pieces so I could chew and swallow them without choking—a fear I always had in the back of my mind.

My steak was tough and my fork weak. As I continued to cut my meat, I could feel the fork bend under my full grip. When I finished cutting, I held my fork up for everyone to see, and the group broke into laughter. Its handle was bowed into what reminded me of a two-year-old's first table utensil.

"Damn fork," I said softly, pretending to put the blame on the eating establishment but failing to keep a straight face.

"I think they need new tableware," Jane offered as a alibi, "but, what the heck, it's northern Wisconsin."

"Hasse, you're just too rough with your stuff," chided Bob. "You're the only guy I know who can murder a fork like that."

George chuckled.

It was fun to have a group of co-workers share in the discovery of a little amusing incident in the happening, feel no embarrassment, and enjoy the resulting camaraderie that spills into everyday work life.

The waitress flitted past George, and he asked for another fork.

I had lost track of the damaged fork during our meal and forgotten about it until George showed up in my office a couple of months later with the plaque. He had swiped the fork from the restaurant and had it mounted.

At the time, I was truly grateful to George. The plaque showed how much the incident, which I had forgotten, meant to him. I was accepted—mumbled speech, crooked back, clanking crutches and all.

I had it hung on the wall across from my woodcut, and an occasional visitor would remark about the odd fork in back of my desk. I would explain about the tough steak, but its significance never really surfaced until I retired to start my second career.

Yes, the fork was a tangible symbol of my acceptance within Heartland Dairies. But the fork's odd curvature began to mean more than that to me as I evaluated my career alternatives at fifty, left Heartland Dairies after twenty-eight years of service, and formed my own home-based communication counseling business.

George, without realizing it, had retrieved a piece of my life that taught me I was more than a person with a disability.

I was physically different, sure. But despite the acceptance I experienced at Heartland Dairies on one level, I was always the odd one in the silverware drawer when it came to personal temperament, outside-work interests, management style, and strategic focus.

That was nothing new. I often didn't fit neatly with others in terms of work, family, friends, lovers, church, and school, or in volunteer efforts and professional organizations. And that didn't matter.

But to give up a successful career—and the apparent security I had—to start my own business was the change in my life many co-workers and relatives just didn't understand. I couldn't explain it adequately to others either, for such a decision contradicted everything I had been trying to achieve since seventh grade: security. I had purposely bent my fork that, in my eyes, had always been straight.

Flying With the Flock

Few things are harder to put up with
than the annoyance of a good example.

—Mark Twain
Pudd'nhead Wilson's Calendar

"I hate people who stare," Pam blurted as we came out of the Goose Neck Cafe, nestled at the edge of Wisconsin's Horicon Marsh. She pretended to say it to me but made sure her voice was loud enough so everyone around the bar inside had heard her.

"Pam!" I scolded in muffled anger as I made my own way to our car. "What are you trying to do? You're only making things worse."

"No, I'm not," she replied loudly, proceeding at her own, quicker pace. "Didn't you see that guy staring at you?"

"No," I said sharply and continued to walk toward our car.

I really hadn't. With crutches cuffed to my forearms, I was too busy trying to negotiate through the clumsy entrance, guarded by a heavy front door.

"I can't get angry every time someone looks at me," I explained in a calmer tone. "Life is too short to get upset about things like that."

"My point is," Pam reasoned, still boiling, "that, if you don't say something, people are never going to realize what they're doing. Doesn't that make you self-conscious?"

"Yeah, it hurts, but they're doing what comes naturally," I shouted back and unlocked the car door. "I'm not out to change the world."

"That's not the point," she insisted. "You need to stand up for yourself."

"Sh-h-h," I said, trying to cover the personal accusation. "I do. But I pick my moments. That was not crucial. There are times when I want to just be—and relax."

I angrily threw my crutches in the back seat and slid under the wheel.

Our day had started with an aimless, relaxing Sunday drive. As one o'clock approached, we, in our serendipity, stopped at the cafe, which popped up along Highway 26.

It was like interrupting a neighborhood Sunday dinner, not normally open to strangers. In a separate room off the bar, we sat down to one of four small tables, topped with plastic tablecloths of red and white squares. Since it was already past noon, the other tables soon became empty.

We had real mashed potatoes and gravy with fried chicken and squash in the room all by ourselves. Only a few regulars sat at the bar across from us. They joshed with the waitress, who also tended the bar and cash register.

After dinner, I proceeded to the rest room, while Pam paid for the meal at the bar.

I squeezed past a bar patron, who was very overweight and filled a stool and a half. The space between his posterior and the wall was so small, I had to proceed sideways, with one of my crutches before me and one after me. Even then, I brushed, ever so slightly, against his broad backside. When I came back from the restroom, I had to go through the same process to get to the front door.

Before going through the front door, I felt an uninhibited urge to take one last look at the patron on the bar stool.

My curiosity overtook me, and I grabbed one quick look—not looking into his face but feasting on his body's bulging profile.

As I started our car, there was dead silence, even though Pam was right next to me.

Suddenly, a racket came from my left. A flock of geese, honking in the empty fall air, had taken off from the marsh in back of the cafe and was beginning to circle and regroup for a fly over the parking lot.

We both got out of the car just in time to catch an overhead glimpse of the flock. The lead goose honked repeatedly as the flock gradually formed a V-shape and flew into the southern wind.

"See!" Pam said, trying to maintain her stern look while unsuccessfully hiding her smile. "Somebody's got to take the lead and make some noise."

"Just making noise is not the answer," I curtly replied. "At some point, you have to decide how you're going to fit in and fly with the flock."

"But don't you feel a responsibility for letting people know how insensitive they can be?" Pam queried in a calmer tone as we drove out of the parking lot and onto Highway 26.

"Not really," I said slowly and glanced one more time at the disappearing flock on the southern horizon. "They all take turns being the lead goose, you know. To be a leader sometimes and a follower at other times takes flexibility."

"That's true."

"Besides, who are we to judge? I found myself doing the same thing we're all upset about. I couldn't help myself. I stared at that overweight man on the stool."

"He looked so bizarre," Pam admitted, almost to herself, with a chuckle.

"See. It's just human nature." I said it. But I didn't feel good about myself as we headed home.

How Does Developing Composure Apply to Your Situation?

1. How have you risen above incidents that could have deflated your self-image?

2. How do you nurture a sense of hope within yourself?

3. How have you dealt with delusions that are seemingly harmless but may be limiting your ability to deal with reality?

4. Under what circumstances do you sacrifice short-term satisfaction for long-term gain?

5. What survival tips have you learned as a person who is different?

6. When is it best for you to forsake security for the excitement of pursuing a calculated risk?

7. Under what circumstances do you willingly become a leader instead of a follower?

Chapter 5

Tasting Success

My Prairie Schooner

The backward look behind the assurance
Of recorded history, the backward half-look
Over the shoulder, towards the primitive terror.
Not fare well,
But fare forward, voyagers.

—T. S. Eliot
Four Quartets

The metal racks of my grocery cart vibrated every time it ran over a seam in the sidewalk as I pushed it to Old Main from my dorm that first morning of classes.

I had placed my books in all four corners of the cart's basket, thinking that arrangement would cut down on the clatter. But the fall air, quiet and heavy with dew, carried the clanking up and down the street.

Already that morning I had walked farther and faster down a street than I had ever gone unaided—without someone else beside me providing balance and protection against pedestrian and auto traffic. That was exhilarating.

But I could feel the quick, curious glances from students on both sides of the street. The grocery cart with its metal baby seat was so noisy it was drawing attention to my disability instead of helping me meld into campus life unnoticed, as I had hoped when I bought it from a grocery store in August.

I cringed as I rolled the cart over another crack in the sidewalk. My feet skipped as I leaned on the cart's handlebar and tried to keep up with the easy roll of the cart's hard, black wheels. I wanted to disappear into the bushes along the sidewalk.

Yet pushing a grocery cart on a relatively flat campus in the prairie land of southwestern Wisconsin was natural for me. It provided me with balance and a convenient way to carry books. That was not obvious, though, to those I met and to those who passed me on the sidewalk that morning.

I slowed the pace of my walk as I maneuvered the cart to the right side of the walkway. A long string of students, a few sporting sweatshirts with "Platteville Pioneers" on the front of them, strutted toward me and passed by. Some smiled. Some didn't. I mentally collected the variety of surprised looks on their faces.

To prove that I was indeed mentally competent and emotionally stable, I greeted the next wave of students with what turned out to be an insecure, " . . . 'Morning."

Some returned the greeting. Most ignored me.

I then tried the detachment of a visionary, ignoring the faces that were walking by me. Yet a few caught my eye, looked at me coldly, and reflected my vagueness. A clanking grocery cart with hard wheels and a freshman with cerebral palsy are not as real, after all, as the past or what was to come.

The future pulled me down the street that morning. I submerged my fear, my shyness, my insecurity, and my embarrassment because I knew my survival was at stake. I had to get through college with good grades to get a good job and break away from farming, the way of life my family had known for three generations—a tradition I could not carry on as the oldest of four children due to my disability.

I also wanted the non-farm life I had come to know while attending grade school in Madison and living with four different families—people ranging from factory workers and janitors to school teachers and business managers.

The past also pushed me in other ways. Images of that past summer's family vacation fluttered through my mind. We had just finished living in the West for seven days as a family of six crammed into a '58 black and white Chevy, tracing the wagon trail of pioneers across the plains into the Rockies.

As we headed east to return home and the Rockies faded in the rear window, we came upon an old prairie schooner, worn and weathered, resting in tall grass along the highway.

Dad stopped the car, and the whole family circled the shell of the wagon. Its ribs, long stripped of covering, reminded me of bones bleached to a dirty gray in the dry sun.

"Pretty crude," Dad said, almost to himself, as he checked the springs on the wagon. "Not much cushion there, but it got the job done."

I pressed my hand against the steel plate on the front of the schooner. Brown and rough with rust, it read, "Robinson Family, Lexington, Kentucky." It stung my palm, reflecting the midday heat.

I imagined the clatter each wheel of the schooner made as it found its way through the flatland. The Robinsons were vulnerable, alone, and defenseless—disconnected from the mainstream of life but self-sufficient and prepared in their quest for a better life.

Finally, I made it to Old Main. My mouth was dry. My chest heaved—partly because I had walked two blocks in the cool, dewy morning air but mostly from the tension of doing something for the first time that was totally different for me. The walk took fifteen minutes, but I had given myself plenty of time to spare in my push into this new territory.

I parked my cart along the stone wall in front of Old Main. It had done its job. The sun glanced off the metal tray from a tea set my sister, Mary, had long outgrown. My mother had attached it to the front of the cart. In black marker, it said. "This belongs to JIM HASSE, handicapped student. Please do not move."

I grabbed my books and held them tight against my chest—using them as counterweights to maintain my balance as I inched myself up the steps to the double doors.

Opening the door, I stumbled into the wide hallway. The echoes of students going to and from class and the musty smell of lockers and newly polished marble floors reminded me of high school back home.

Ground Not Covered

The art of being wise is the art of knowing what to overlook.

—William James
The Principles of Psychology

"You want to take this Spanish course?" asked Professor Roder in precise diction. He took a quick glance over his reading glasses at my twisted torso. "How can you? You can't even speak English clearly."

"Dat's . . . dat's true," I stammered. My fractured speech crackled in the muffled silence of the language lab. "But I'm in . . . I'm in Letters and Science — pre-journalism."

"Hm-m-m," he said almost to himself, folding his arms across a belly that protruded beyond his black belt.

"I need a foreign language," I said weakly, trying to fill the awkward silence.

Professor Roder looked at me again. This time our eyes met. "I have cerebral palsy," I said more confidently, anticipating his next question.

"Well—" he stalled, grabbing his fleshy jowl with his right hand. I could tell his mind was racing to fathom all the possible problems or predicaments he had never faced before.

He was a big, roly-poly man in a black, ill-fitting suit and an unironed white shirt. His graying hair, which covered only the sides and back of his balding head, needed combing. How could a man with such a sloppy appearance become a professor of languages?

I watched with envy as his lips moved effortlessly and precisely when he finally said, "Let me think more about it. I"ll get back to you on Thursday."

"Thanks," I said, glad he was going to at least give my circumstances some thought. At the same time, I was concerned about how I was going to get through his course with a passing grade. "I'd really appreciate any help you can give me."

I stumbled back to my cubicle and placed the headset over my ears just like the other twelve students in Spanish 101. My first day of class as a sophomore at Platteville State University was about to begin.

The earphones didn't bother me. It was the microphone in front me that made me squirm. How could I roll my "r's" with others in the class when I couldn't even pronounce the "th" sound in English correctly? I didn't say a word throughout the whole class that first day as the others began their first drills.

"¿Hablas español? ¡Sí, hablo español! ¿Hablas español? ¡Sí, hablo español! ¿Hablas español? ¡Sí, hablo español!"

The first drills reminded me of the long rows of hay Dad and I had baled that summer on our farm of rolling hills in south-central Wisconsin. Strapped to the seat of our 540 IH tractor so I would not fall off, I would put the tractor in third gear and guide it down the windrow with the baler behind the tractor and the wagon behind the baler.

The baler would spit out bales of hay, bound by binder

twine, and kick them back into the three-sided wagon, where Dad would retrieve them and stack them neatly into rows.

Baling in the flat was enjoyable at first but soon became boring as the baler repeatedly would gobble up the hay. Then it would throw out a finished bale with a "chunk . . . chunk . . . chunk" sound.

But turning the corner at the end of rows on the hillsides was not boring. It was more frightening and more dangerous than on the level because the strips of hay followed the contours of the field. Despite power steering on the tractor, I would sometimes swing too wide on the corners and miss part of the windrow.

Disgusted, Dad would stand on the wagon, motioning me to cut my corners shorter.

After all the windrows in a field were gone, I would compensate for my sloppy turns and chase down the little wisps of hay I had left behind at the corners. And Dad would stand on the wagon, shaking his head about the extra time and energy I was using to gather the bits of hay I should have gotten on the first go-around.

But keeping up with the drills in Spanish class that first day of class was even more frightening than baling hay on hilly land. How could I keep up with a class that kept moving into progressively more complicated phases and put so much emphasis on verbal skill? By the end of the hour, my mind was numb and my head was pounding.

On Thursday, dressed in the same sloppy, black suit, Professor Roder came to the lab with another question about my predicament. "Why are you taking this course, Mr. Hasse?" he demanded.

"It's a requirement," I again repeated without thinking.

"Is that the only reason?" he pumped. I felt my whole body stiffen.

"I'm going . . . into j-j-journalism," I finally got out.

"So why do you need Spanish for journalism?" he again asked. He looked me in the eye. A frown had appeared between his bushy, black eyebrows.

"To learn how to write better?" My response was more question than answer.

"You got it," he almost shouted and his puffy face brightened. "Learning a second language will help you write well in English. You'll learn how the English language works. I'm willing to forego the verbal requirement of this course in your case. I'll grade you on your written work."

"That's fine," I agreed, amazed at the extra edge he was giving me just because of my disability.

I was relieved that my predicament had been resolved. At the same time, I was uncomfortable, knowing that I was getting a break others in the class would not receive. Even in 1962, the level playing field was not really level. And it could be tilted both ways, depending on an individual's own circumstances.

I studied hard for the course and did well on the written exams, but I couldn't compensate for the fact that Professor Roder had tilted the field in my favor.

For the semester, I received a "B" in Spanish 101.

Mistaken Identities

Two o'clock in the morning courage:
I mean unprepared courage.

—Napoleon Bonaparte
Las Cases

The telephone rang, and I hopped naked across the bed to the wall phone next to my dresser. I grabbed it on the fourth ring and flipped on the light switch.

"Hello," I said, my breathless voice cracking. I glanced at the clock beside my bed. It was 1:30 A.M., and I had just gotten to sleep after a four-hour study marathon for an exam on Monday.

No answer.

"Hello," I repeated, this time a little louder and probably with a clearer voice but still out of breath from getting my stiff body across the room to answer the phone. The gray, tiled floor was cold and I propped my left foot against my right leg to warm my toes.

"Is Ken there?" a man's tentative voice finally asked.

"No . . . he isn't," I said slowly, trying to make myself understood. "He should be back pretty soon."

It was Friday night, and I could hear the band still playing the last strains of "Louie, Louie" in the dorm's basement below me.

"Is this 117 Sullivan Hall?"

"Yes."

"Who is this?"

"I'm Jim Hasse. I'm Ken's roommate." The crowd below threw up a cheer. Apparently the band's last set had ended.

"Whooo?" he yelled.

"K-e-n-'s r-o-o-m-m-a-t-e," I found myself shouting louder and slower, which only made my garbled speech more noticeable. "J-i-m H-a-s-s-e."

"Well, Jim Hasse, can you have Ken call me as soon as he gets back?"

"Sure," I said, relieved he understood but puzzled by his cockiness.

"Tell him to call Cal Lewis at 367-9596." I didn't have a pencil or a piece of paper in front of me, but I visualized the name and number in my mind so I could write it down later.

"Can you repeat that to me?"

"Cal Lewis. 367-9596."

"Be sure to tell him to call me," he demanded.

"I will."

I hung up the phone and scrambled across the room to jot down the name and telephone number at my desk and left it there. I then crawled across my bed to turn off the light.

It seemed I had just fallen asleep when the telephone rang again. I whipped off the covers and bounded over them to the phone. This time I didn't bother with the lights. My heavy eyelids kept falling shut.

"Hello."

"Hi, guy. Ken back yet?" I recognized Cal's voice again, although he didn't identify himself.

"No." Across the room, my digital clock beamed "1:45" in a green glow.

"Remember to have Ken call me," Cal demanded. "Do you still have my number?"

"Yeah."

"What is it?"

"Ah . . . ahh . . . 3-5-6 - 9-5-9-6," I recited, trying desperately to recall.

"It's 367-9596, you son-of-a-bitch! Write it down."

"I did. It's on my desk."

"Like shit you did," he sneered. "Hey, buddy, you be sure to have him call me, you hear?"

"I will," I yelled, slammed the phone back onto the wall unit and crawled back into bed.

I woke up again as Ken came creeping into our room without turning on the lights, trying not to disturb me.

"Might as well turn on the lights," I moaned without moving in my bed.

"Why?"

"Some drunk has been trying to call you. He called twice. Cal Lewis. His number's on my desk."

Ken flipped on the lights, retrieved the number from my desk and dialed the phone.

"Cal?" he asked in a muffled voice, as though speaking softly would further prevent disruption of my sleep. But I was now too curious to sleep. "What's up?

The dorm was still with a quiet that only comes with the early morning hours.

I watched Ken unbutton his shirt as he cradled the phone on his shoulder.

"Huh. Yeah. Well . . . let's see . . . I can meet you tomorrow. How about lunch—say, about 12:30 at the Pub? Fine." Pause. Ken chuckled nervously, and his face turned red. "I'll talk to you tomorrow. Good night."

He hung up the phone and broke out in a full belly laugh. I sat up in bed.

"Well, what?"

"That was my ROTC instructor. He thought YOU were drunk."

I laughed, too, with relief and gratitude. I was glad that Ken could see the humor in the situation and share it with me, for it was a true test. He accepted me for what I was. He understood.

As he turned out the light, my eyes were no longer sleepy. I had met the real world that night. I wondered how I would cope with such unknown pitfalls after graduation when I was no longer Ken's roommate in 117 Sullivan Hall.

Hot Type, Cold Reality

Life is the game that must be played:
This truth at least, good friends, we know;
So live and laugh, nor be dismayed
As one by one the phantoms go.

—Edwin Arlington Robinson
Ballade by the Fire

The wide poster was the first thing I saw as I walked into the men's room.

The blonde stood there at the urinal, her backside to her intended audience—in calf-length black boots, tight, black leather mini-skirt, and red, free-flowing blouse. With both hands in front of her, she looked down into the drain and appeared to be urinating just like the man three urinals to her left.

Her male counterpart in the poster, brawny and dark-haired, duplicated her stance. Dressed in khakis and red-and-blue striped shirt, he glanced at her out of his right eye, unruffled but curious.

The four-color poster of this unisex restroom scene was carefully taped to the off-white concrete block and covered the wall above two of the restroom's urinals, stained brown with a continual trickle of rusty water and years of haphazard cleaning.

As I stood there—relieving myself—with my face six inches from the woman's perfectly proportioned thighs, I found the copyright in small print at the right-hand, lower corner of the four-color poster: Calco Productions 1965.

This was my first day on the job and my first trip to the men's restroom at the central office of Heartland Dairies at Prairie Center, a rural area of the Badger State. Some people, I later learned, liked to call this "the armpit of Wisconsin."

I wondered who had placed the poster in the men's room. But I didn't ask.

And I wondered what Lonnie, the receptionist with melting blue eyes and a body the men in the office ogled over, thought of the poster. Or maybe she didn't know.

Behind closed doors but just fifteen feet from Lonnie's desk, the poster daily reinforced the silliness that the male employees probably associated with the women's movement that was taking shape throughout the country.

"Mr. Firstle is not at his desk right now," Lonnie answered the telephone. I didn't take much stock in that exchange until I heard the women refer to Mr. Harland, Mr. Sands, etc. during their coffee break.

Lonnie and the other clerical staff workers—all female—were losing a silent battle within the second-story, brick office of a pre-World War II milk-drying plant, and they didn't know it.

In the hallway I recognized Boyd, production director, as he slipped out of his office with another man behind him.

"This is Jim Hasse, who will be working with Sid Turner on our newsletter," Boyd announced, as he introduced me to Carl, chairman of the board. "Jim has done what most of us haven't had a chance to do—graduate from college. He took journalism at the UW-Madison."

I shook Carl's hand, a broad, calloused palm developed only through years of manual labor as a farmer.

"Hello," I said. "I'm very glad to be here."

I chose a string of wrong words, and they came out garbled.

Carl didn't understand but covered the awkward moment eloquently. "Well, welcome to Heartland Dairies. We'll be watching what you do with the *Heartland Report*."

I went back to my manual typewriter and my desk, a folding card table outside the office's coffee room. The room, large enough to seat eight, had cookies, candy, and coffee. But it was an area, I noticed, men in management didn't visit.

The deadline for the October, 1965 *Heartland Report* was less than a week away. I shuffled through the stack of dairy magazines, daily newspapers, and USDA reports Sid had given me to scan before our visit to the local newspaper office where the newsletter was printed.

Halfway through the stack, I discovered a joke book for speakers, yellowed and tattered, that various people had apparently saved through the years. I scanned the pages to see if it contained anything appropriate as a filler for the upcoming newsletter.

I came up empty because most of the jokes poked fun at women, African-Americans or people with disabilities—in about that order.

But I decided to keep the little book, which was dated 1956, with the hope I could use some of the material by changing the characters involved but retaining the essence of the humor. It would be difficult but could keep my creative juices going.

Sid and I drove into town where he introduced me to Wally, the local printer who also published the weekly newspaper. A graying man with a crew cut, Wally was still using hot type for his newspaper and the *Heartland Report*. That shouldn't have surprised me.

I had looked at the previous month's newsletter and wondered why the printing was so poor. Two photos, each showing a 4-H'er with a prize calf at the local fair, stretched across two columns of the first page, but they were crooked, not quite perpendicular to each other.

"A little drinking problem there," Sid told me on the way back to the office. "But catch him when he's sober, and he does a pretty good job."

Through college, I had dreamed of working in an advertising agency on Chicago's Wacker Drive. Instead, I ended up in the "armpit of Wisconsin." Was this the fate of a person with a disability who had graduated with honors from the UW-Madison's School of Journalism?

It would be easy to show improvement in the newsletter after just a couple of months. Or was that expecting too much? I didn't realize it then, but my education had just begun.

Preferences

. . . It is not wisdom to be only wise,
And on the inward vision close the eyes,
But it is wisdom to believe the heart . . .

—George Santayana
O World, Thou Choosest Not

Fascinated by the preciseness of his animated fingers, I stuck my hand out in front of me and tried to mimic his gestures in the shadows of the theater. But I only saw a gnarled hand—thick and crippled with crooked fingers that didn't obey my command to replicate the subtlety of his silent expression.

I had first noticed him when he sat down with a female companion four rows ahead of me in the Memorial Union theater. All I could see was the profile of his face and his hand that popped up into view as he checked the time on his watch. Yes, fifteen minutes until curtain time, I confirmed, glancing at my own watch.

Pretending not to stare at him, I tried to focus on the people coming into the theater. But—again—his animated hand, gracefully accenting the conversation he was having with his companion, drew my attention.

He had long, slender fingers—perhaps those of a conductor or a pianist. His wrist first pivoted clockwise and then counter-clockwise. His fingers punctuated the black backdrop of the stage with an array of patterns, which had a rhythm all their own.

Trying to pivot my own wrist and form my thumb and fingers into a crown like his, I only produced a jerky movement, which grew even more grotesque after my fourth attempt. I finally closed my hand and stuck it into my suit pocket.

As couples and foursomes started filing into the theater, the combined chatter of a Saturday-night-out grew louder. Two couples quickly filled the row where I was sitting and began to tease one another about last Friday night's party.

I was still focused on the pianist four rows ahead of me. His forefinger momentarily came to rest on his temple. He looked at his partner, a slender-faced brunette with long eyelashes, and I could see love in his gestures. His fingertips again happily pierced the darkness under the soft spotlight from the ceiling.

I felt hollow inside my chest. At twenty-three, I was still going through the self-doubts normally experienced by a thirteen-year-old. Why is it so difficult to love and be loved when you don't conform with what the current culture considers the norm?

"You may marry someday," my mother had always told me. "But whoever you marry will have to be someone very special, and she's going to have to love you very much," she would say.

She wouldn't say it, but I knew what she meant. It would have to be someone who didn't mind my disability.

I was more idealistic than that. True—I was not nimble physically, but what counted was the kind of person I was and whether my spirit, values, and interests had a good match with my partner. That match was the important element of a relationship. Preferences. Possibilities. To me, both were passports to happiness.

Yet I did not hear that approach to relationships reaffirmed in rural Wisconsin during the early '60s.

I remember a conservative Lutheran pastor, a close family friend, fuming about his daughter's decision to marry a man who used a wheelchair. "It was her choice," he would say under his breath, "to marry a cripple. But apparently they're happy."

I was amused whenever he would repeat his sentiments about his daughter's marriage. He was genuine in his surprise that they may be happy together—that they would prefer each other and each find the other attractive, charming, and fascinating.

The theater's lights gradually grew dimmer, and the curtain parted on stage, revealing the string quartet from Julliard.

Amid the applause of the audience, the woman closest to me in my row eyed the empty seat between us.

"Is this taken?" she whispered.

"No," I answered sheepishly.

She placed her shawl neatly on the seat next to me.

Bungled Bluff

Mishaps are like knives, that either serve us or cut us, as we grasp them by the blade or the handle.

—James Russell Lowell
Literary Essays

"Bob, I'd like to meet with you and Jim sometime this week," Jeff inserted into the closing pleasantries of our monthly meeting with the president. His baritone voice was strained, and our group of four, gathered around Bob's desk, suddenly became silent.

"Jim and I have a disagreement over work schedules," Jeff continued. Judy, Jeff's counterpart in public relations within my department, dropped her jaw in disbelief. Bob, with no knowledge of what Jeff was talking about, narrowed his lips.

I felt a twitch go through my neck. I couldn't believe Jeff was going through with his threat of going to the president with an issue I had often said was not negotiable.

"OK. How about Thursday at 1:30?" Bob said. He seemed confused but open to the request.

"Fine," Jeff replied quickly. "How's that for you, Jim?"

"That'll work for me, Bob," I said in scrambled vowel sounds. I ignored Jeff and, instead, looked Bob directly in the eye. Bob glanced at me, then his eyes began to flit along the expanse of windows surrounding his corner office. I reached for my crutches as Jeff and Judy left the room, and then I saw the frown on Bob's forehead.

"I need to fill you in on what's happening here," I said quietly. "I thought Jeff and I could iron out the issues between us, but apparently he doesn't think so. Could I meet with you briefly later this afternoon on this matter?"

"That would be helpful," Bob said stiffly. "I've got a 4:30 open."

"Fine," I said. "I'll outline where we are on all this."

As I walked out of his office, I scolded myself for not giving Bob some forewarning that, for several days, Jeff had been threatening to bring our disagreement about his workload and compensation to Bob's attention. He felt I was being unfair, and he needed someone at the next level of authority to resolve the two issues. But I never thought he would actually request a meeting with Bob about them.

I kept telling Jeff that it would be a mistake, that it wasn't how issues were resolved in our corporate culture. Deep down, I knew it would be political suicide for Jeff and hurt my image as a manager and a leader in Bob's eyes—especially because I walked and talked with difficulty.

I could feel the pressure to keep proving I had the moxie to manage people. It hung in the air every time I walked into the executive wing.

"Jeff believes his workload is too heavy," I told Bob bluntly that afternoon. "We keep records of our time by project in our department. It's true that he's putting in about fifty-five hours a week, but we all do."

"So what's the problem?" Bob asked. I saw the faint lines of the frown on his forehead begin to deepen.

"Well, he and his wife have a new baby daughter at home," I said. "He'd like to spend more time with them. And he's comparing his salary with other publication editors in the area—claims we're not competitive. I've told him that a mid-year adjustment is not in the cards."

"So why are you two coming to me?"

"I didn't expect him to bring these issues to your attention. He probably needs to hear it from you," I admitted, realizing as an afterthought how weak that sounded to Bob.

"And I want to hear what he has to say," Bob confirmed. His tone had an edge that was open, yet troubling. I left his office not sure what to expect when we met again with Jeff on Thursday.

I didn't understand Jeff's lack of political acumen. Didn't he understand that making me appear ineffective in front of my boss was one of the basic mistakes to avoid? It was 1979. Maybe he was a child of the '60s and never really grew out of its rebellion.

Or did he believe I was a pushover—that somehow due to my physical disability, he could ignore the conventional pattern of dealing with me as his immediate supervisor? Did he think he could gain the upper hand by going over my head?

As communication director, I had hired Jeff four years before, after he had worked in an electrical utility's public relations department. Because he was a good writer, I had chosen him to edit our internal and external publications.

Even though his resume listed a B.S. degree in journalism, I had received rumors that he, in fact, had not completed his studies toward a degree. Was he prone to taking short cuts when the going got tough?

Was escalating a disagreement into an issue which had to be considered by the company president a symptom of a larger problem in how he approached life?

Jeff began Thursday's meeting by showing Bob his time sheets, a smattering of figures that I knew Bob wouldn't absorb. Bob liked short, verbal summaries of a situation. I could see the blood rise in his face.

"I'm not being paid a competitive salary for a job that is taking in excess of fifty-five hours a week," Jeff summarized, "and Jim refuses to do anything at all to address this situation."

Bob shifted himself in his black leather executive chair. His face was red, but his lips grew white as he pursed them before he spoke.

"I know what it's like to start a family on a limited income and work long hours doing it," he finally said in a controlled, tense voice. "I've done it myself."

"I understand that, Bob," Jeff agreed. "But . . . "

"Essentially, you're doing the same job Jim did before you came," Bob broke in. "Is that not right, Jim?"

"That's right," I concurred.

"But that's not the case," Jeff objected, taking a quick swipe with his right hand through his long, black hair that curled to his collar. "Jim has added so many other things to my job in the last year that . . . "

"Jeff, that's not true," I broke in, trying to calm the situation but get my point of view across. Bob's face was getting redder. "It's the same job . . . "

"But you're single, and you were putting in sixty to seventy hours a week . . . "

"OK, guys. I've heard all I'm going to hear from both of you," Bob blurted out. "You realize I have never had to deal with this kind of thing in the other four departments? I spend more time with you people than any other group."

"You're right, Bob," I agreed humbly. "You shouldn't have to spend time on this issue."

"I felt this was my only recourse, Bob," Jeff said boldly. "Jim's not addressing the situation."

"We don't adjust salaries in mid-year." Bob stated bluntly. "It's up to you two to resolve the workload issue."

With a shrug, Jeff left Bob's office.

"I've got to be candid with you, Jim," Bob said in a milder manner. "I'm asking myself, 'Do you really have what it takes to manage people?'"

"I believe I do," I stated weakly. "This was just an end run I didn't see coming."

"Well, let's see how you handle this situation," he said.

"I'll handle it," I said more confidently. I retrieved the crutches from underneath my chair and stumbled out of Bob's office.

I continued to meet weekly with Jeff, asking him to explore ways to make his time on the job more productive. Our sessions would invariably end with a restatement of his objections about his work situation. In reply, I would repeat what was becoming a litany for me: "I'm not going to change the responsibilities or the salary for this position. You have a choice—decide to work within these requirements at this salary level or find another opportunity that's more suitable to you."

Within three months, Jeff finally announced he was leaving to write for a newspaper.

Jeff apparently was telling others about our sessions, which I considered confidential. They must have been a favorite item on the office grapevine, for, as I would walk through the hallways with the soft rubber tips of my crutches bouncing off the red brick floor, my co-workers would, at times, curiously ask, "How are things going?"

The grapevine had apparently also reached the corner office of the executive wing. During my mid-year review, Bob admitted, "You've shown you can be consistent in managing people."

How Does Tasting Success Apply to Your Situation?

1. In what ways have you risen above difficult situations and put them into perspective?

2. How do you decide what is critical and what is not so critical to your long-term success?

3. What circumstances have given you the opportunity to face reality about how others often perceive you and to deal with that reality?

4. At what times have you accepted people for who they are and situations for what potential they offered?

5. How does your own personal vision drive your thoughts and actions?

6. In what ways have you proven to people that their original expectations of your capabilities were too low?

Chapter 6
Obtaining Balance

For Those Who Need Help Making It

Your life will be rich for others only as it is rich for you.

—David McCord
On the Frontiers of Understanding

I've endured the indifference of Nassau, basked in the anonymity of New York, and marveled at the brashness of Paris, but in the struggle for life on East Africa's Serengeti Plain, I've felt the pulse of humanity.

Toka, our guide for the day, took a sharp left turn to get our Land Rover into the groove of the track leading to the rim of the small, long-dead crater we could see in the distance. Dust flew out of the back end of the vehicle, a crude cross between a VW minibus and a U.S. Army Jeep, as we sped toward the cavity that pocked an otherwise flat land.

"We go see elephant," Toka told our group of seven, all Wisconsinites on a 1973 People-to-People tour of East Africa. He pointed to the approaching crater on the northeastern horizon. "Last week, we saw three."

My crutches began to dance around on the floor of the Rover as it bounced over the rough track. I kicked my left foot against them to brace them against the back of the driver's seat.

I was intrigued by Toka's right ear lobe. Apparently elongated since his childhood, his lobe could be wrapped around his ear and tucked neatly in back of where his ear lobe normally would have been if it hadn't been stretched.

Toka was a Masai but had forsaken the nomadic traditions of his people to become a guide for Serengeti National Park in Tanzania. His father hunted with a spear, and now Toka was driving a Rover with a rifle strapped to the door beside him.

As we suddenly veered off the track for no apparent reason, I grabbed the back of Toka's driver's seat for support. My crutches slid to the other side of the Rover, thudding against the right side door. He glanced at me with his deep brown eyes, and I smiled to indicate it was OK.

Then I saw the carcass. The vultures feeding on the rhino flew up over our Land Rover as we drew closer and circled the body. The lifeless hide looked hollow and small compared to the snout.

"Poachers," he exclaimed, pointing to the missing horns—a detail I would have missed if he hadn't pointed it out. He shook his head as we returned to the track, hopping across tire grooves in the earth made by an earlier vehicle while the soil was still soggy.

As we jostled in the Rover, I watched Toka's ear and wondered how he kept his elongated ear lobe in place. I also marveled at Toka's adaptability—how he had made the jump from nomad to guide. But how will he cope as his corner of the world opens up to more poachers with no sense of responsibility and more tourists with a pretentiousness not useful in East Africa? How will he handle more travelers with mobility problems in a land where convenience is not yet a necessity?

The bumpy track turned into a gravel road, smoother and less dusty. Toka was alternately watching the road and searching the northwestern horizon into what seemed endless miles of flatland.

"Wildebeest," he announced matter-of-factly to our group and pointed to a small, rising cloud of dust that was approaching the road ahead of us. As we continued down the road, we soon began to see the faint outlines of the charging herd.

"Dry season now," Toka explained. "Wildebeest go to higher ground. More water."

I could see they were eventually going to cross the road in front of us.

But I was unprepared for the stampede that surrounded our Rover as we plunged northward in third gear. Toka seemed unconcerned. The wildebeest, pounding the Serengeti floor and stirring up clouds of dust on a full run, avoided our vehicle as we plowed ahead. We opened our own hole in the herd as it crossed the road in front of us. Their odd, bearded, buffalo heads seemed too large for their horse-like bodies.

Here and there, yearling calves—smaller, more tan than brown and without beards—crossed in front and in back of us. And then there were the more mature bulls—less agile but still able to keep up with the herd.

Suddenly, it was over. It was quiet, except for the grinding of our Rover toward the crater and our hopes of seeing elephants.

As we again left the road and started a gradual incline to the crater's rim, we passed another rack of bones. It was a wildebeest, Toka said, which didn't make it. The bones, bleached to a sickening gray, had been picked clean by jackals and hyenas.

At the base of the crater, Toka parked the Rover under the acacia tree's broad, drooping branches and pointed to what appeared to me an ordinary hill above us. It was a short walk up a fairly steep incline dotted with short shrubs.

I retrieved my crutches from the floor of the Rover and proceeded up the rim, but I soon fell behind the others in our group who were anxious to see their first glimpse of an elephant in the wild. I felt confident I could make it, but I knew it would take some time.

Toka came up behind me and tapped me on my shoulder.

"Ride?" he asked and pointed to his back.

I declined. I knew I could make it on my own, but he persisted.

"I know," Toka said. I could see earnestness and understanding in his eyes.

He took my crutches, laid them on the ground, and hoisted me onto his back. I wrapped my arms around his neck and my feet around his haunches.

Toka was not a big man by Western standards, but we made it up the hill, just in time for him to meet our group on the rim. He helped them quietly look down into the crater's wide, shallow floor and pointed out two elephants, surprisingly close, dwarfing the acacia trees around them.

First Intimacy

My valor is certainly going! It is sneaking off! I feel it oozing out, as it were, at the palm of my hands!

—Richard Brinsley Sheridan
The Rivals

"We should be at the theater in twenty minutes," I said. "Let's eat in the car."

I drove up to Burger King so Shelly and I could grab a quick bite to eat before the Friday night concert. We were still wearing our office garb.

"What are you going to have?" the counter person asked Shelly through the speaker system.

"Let's see—double burger with bacon, tomato, onion," she announced.

"Catsup?"

"No, mayo, please"

"Anything else?"

"Large fries and medium Diet Coke."

"How about you, sir?"

"I'm just going to just have a hamburger," I said, almost to myself.

"Anything on it? Mayo, catsup, tomato, onions, lettuce, bacon?"

"Uh—yeah—give it the works. And a Coke."

"Small, medium, or large?"

"Medium."

"Anything else?"

"That's all."

"That'll be $5.98. Please drive up to the next window."

"So many choices," I said to Shelly. "What ever happened to the good old-fashioned hamburger?"

It was our fifth date, and we were becoming comfortable together—starting to feel safe in revealing little hints of idiosyncrasies to each other and having fun doing it.

"If you wanted a plain hamburger," she said softly, "all you had to do was just ask. This is build-your-own burger territory."

"Too complicated," I replied with my alibi, as I paid for our sack meals, handed them to Shelly, and carefully placed our covered Cokes on the console.

I felt good about my small string of successes. Despite my slurred speech, the counter person understood my order. I received change for my ten-dollar bill without dropping it between my seat and the door on the driver's side. And I got the Cokes into the car without crushing them.

I parked the car so we could watch the sunset across Burger King's half-filled lot.

We slid our seats back, and I grabbed several napkins to place across my lap.

"This is what I call dining out," I cracked as I pushed two buttons to open the front windows and turned on the radio to a soft concerto. The fresh spring air mingled with the burger aroma.

I didn't know I was in trouble until I unwrapped my sandwich. It was huge and contained a conglomeration of pickles, tomato, lettuce, and mayo with two hamburger patties on a mushy hamburger bun.

I tried to rewrap it, thinking the wrapper would help me hold it together. But the more I struggled with it, the flimsier the bun became.

Finally, I clenched both fists around the burger and took a bite. Pickles and mayo oozed out of each side. My fingers suddenly had a mind of their own and tried to contain the mess.

"Help," I said frantically because I did not want to get this mess on my suit.

Shelly looked at me and didn't know what to do.

This is ridiculous, I told myself, fighting back shame and embarrassment.

"Help," I again said in a tone I hoped would convey the urgency of my predicament and, at the same time, my willingness to laugh about the situation.

"How can I help?" Shelly finally said in a calm manner that surprised me. She had a puzzled smirk on her face. "I don't know what to do."

"Just take this," I explained. "It's too big. I can't handle it."

My fingers relaxed as she took the wrapper with the mangled hamburger from my hands. We giggled, each knowing we had learned something new about the other.

"Can you break it into two?" I asked, reverting back to my analytical nature. "Just hand it to me in smaller chunks, and I can do it."

"Jim," she said softly. "All you had to do was just ask."

Blind Discovery

Even in the common affairs of life, in love, friendship, and marriage, how little security have we when we trust our happiness in the hands of others!

—William Hazlitt
On Living to One's Self

Forty years of living had prepared me for this moment. I didn't realize it then, but I was about to meet and recognize a fellow traveler for the first time.

I sat there on the hard, wooden chair, calm but brimming with anticipation—so involved with my own dread of yet another polite but stiff evening with a blind date that my eyes rested blankly on the carpeting of the reception area. The thick carpeting had muffled her approach, and she caught me off guard.

"Jim?" I heard a woman's voice say. I looked up and saw Pam's broad smile, highlighted by red lipstick.

"Oh, yeah," I answered clumsily and struggled to stand up to introduce myself. "Jim Hasse. You're Pam?"

"That's right," she said, still smiling. She was petite and wore a blue suit. I shook her right hand, a hand so small it covered only half of my palm. Her right wrist was scarred and came out of her sleeve at an odd angle.

"Well, welcome to the Cobblestone Supper Club," I said lightly. It seemed the natural thing to say, since I had arrived first.

It was 7:10 by my watch. Being ten minutes late was only a minor annoyance, but I had learned to pick up on the little things on blind dates. Besides, I had been stood up several times on previous dates with women I had only met by telephone and never heard from again after waiting a half hour—or even an hour—and finally going home, alone and depressed.

"Let's get a booth," I suggested, relieved that at least I had made all the right connections. Pam was there, apparently accepting my invitation to dinner.

I retrieved my crutches from the floor, and we followed the *maitre d'* to the booth I had reserved. I noticed a slight wobble in Pam's gait as we left the reception area. The cleats on her heels clacked and my aluminum crutches clanked along the cobblestone floor, raising a clatter that caused the diners in the next booth to glance up and take notice.

"I have cerebral palsy," I said matter-of-factly after we settled into our booth. Women, I had found, generally were impressed by my willingness to be up front with them. "If you don't understand me, just say so. I'll repeat . . . "

"I know."

"Have had it since birth," I said, adding a detail in anticipation of the next question that always seemed to follow such an admission.

"I know," Pam repeated in what seemed to be a slight German accent.

I was curious about the letter I had received from her. It only read, "I work with a man who knows a friend of yours. I would very much like to meet you. Pam. 322-9836." So I called Pam and asked her to join me for dinner, a ritual I had mastered during my middle-age efforts to gain a social life.

"How did you get my name?" I bluntly asked.

"I'm a nursing assistant at the clinic on campus," Pam explained, in a louder-than-normal voice. "Professor Amato knows someone you used to go out with."

"Carol?" I asked, still not clear about the connections.

"Some nurse—I'm not sure," Pam conceded, although I felt she knew more than she was telling me. Her eyes met mine and then came to rest on her wine glass. They were soft, hazel eyes that sparkled every time she talked.

"What does he do?"

"Professor Amato?

"Yeah."

"He's a psychotherapist for the clinic," Pam recounted. "Part-time. He also does counseling at St. Luke's."

That was the guy Carol had been telling me about. They worked together at the same hospital in town.

"We broke up," I finally said. " . . . I mean Carol and I. She was going off in weird directions. Told me no one man could meet her needs. She went back to Tennessee."

"To where?" Pam asked, again apparently not understanding me.

"To Tennessee," I repeated more slowly.

"Yeah, that's what he said," Pam allowed.

We ordered two glasses of Chablis.

"Are psychotherapists allowed to be matchmakers?" I asked almost to myself, both annoyed and surprised that a bit of my personal life was being discussed by strangers.

"Professor Amato is a close friend of mine," Pam replied to what she apparently took as a cross-examination. "He just mailed me a note, saying I might like to meet you."

We both became preoccupied with our wine glasses.

"Carol said I would never meet anyone like her again,"

I suddenly admitted, realizing I was violating one of the basic rules of meeting someone new. I never discussed other relationships—especially on a first date.

"Once I had a guy say the same thing to me," Pam offered in a lower, more intimate voice. "But that was a long time ago. We were engaged, but I just couldn't go through with it. I broke it off. I felt so guilty."

"Like it's your fault," I added, recalling my own experience with Carol.

"It just didn't feel right. I was twenty at the time. Wasn't ready to get married. But my sister was really mad at me. She said it was my last chance." Pam grinned.

"Your last chance?" I repeated with a chuckle. "At twenty?"

"My mother didn't like him," Pam added, "because he wore white socks."

"I wore white socks back then," I admitted. "They were in—at least for me."

"But she didn't understand that."

"I only started dating five years ago," I stated, realizing I was revealing a fact about my life I had not put into words before. "Too occupied with my job. I decided I needed a balance."

"What do you do?"

"I'm communication director for Heartland Dairies," I recounted automatically, glad to switch to a more comfortable topic. "I do public relations, member communication, employee relations—that sort of thing. There are five of us in the department."

That didn't seem to impress her much. She began looking at the menu. I decided to do the same. She ordered the northern pike; I decided on the tenderloin tips.

"Anyway," I continued in an effort to reconnect again by switching back to a discussion of relationships in general, "I've found life doesn't end at twenty. It's just a different game when you're older."

"I don't know if it's a game," she slowly questioned, again reverting to her louder-than-normal voice. Her eyes opened wider. She did not blink.

"Dating, I mean," I explained, disappointed that what I thought was insightful came across as a platitude. "It can be a bitch."

"Oh, that's true," she allowed, more reflectively, and her eyes mellowed. "Especially at middle age."

"I've dated one person who is suicidal," I related. "Two were obsessed by their fathers, and I just didn't measure up. One was so intellectual she was cold. It was like she had no feelings. Another was a manic-depressive . . . "

"I see you've been around," she interrupted with laughter. "I once went with a guy who I suspect was gay, but that doesn't match your record . . . "

"Seems like not one of them has figured out what life is all about."

"Have you?"

"No . . . " I quickly added, surprised at her directness. "I'm still working on that one."

Our food came. I went through the motions of eating my meal without really tasting it, concentrating, instead, on a conversation that had not become the guarded chatter I usually encountered on first dates.

"Anyway," I continued, "how can you build a relationship with a person, if you don't know who you are?"

"I don't know," Pam replied. "That's why I've come to the point where I'm comfortable living alone. I used to live with various groups of girls when I first started working, and at the time I dreaded the thought of living alone. But group living gets old. Now I have my own apartment, and it works."

"I know what you mean," I added, trying to prove I was also independent. "I bought a condo four years ago. Living alone has its advantages . . . "

" . . . and disadvantages," she admitted. "It can be lonely. Don't you sometimes feel you're missing something?"

"Yeah," I agreed, finding myself mentally running to keep up with her. "But it's better than living with someone who isn't on your wave length."

"The more I think about it, the more I think we've got this marriage thing all wrong," Pam said more softly and slowly. "Two can't become one. You're still two separate individuals."

I could see I was a bit more idealistic. "But the right two people together can create a third dimension that is greater than just putting two people together and calling them a couple," I tried to explain. It was 1983—before corporate commercials on Sunday morning TV had made *synergy* a household word.

"Maybe."

We both concentrated on our food.

"You can lose your individuality so easily," Pam said, breaking the silence that didn't seem awkward but, instead, became another means of sharing. "That's what scares me."

Our conversation floated through a second glass of wine and dessert.

It was over coffee that Pam broke the cadence of our conversation with more firmness in her voice. "There's something I must tell you," she insisted, citing what I had surmised. "I have cerebral palsy, too. I was premature and have always been deaf on my left side."

"I understand," I assured her, then realizing why she tended to skip some consonants and soften certain vowels in a voice that tended to be louder than normal. I could see relief sweep over her face. "But what happened to your hand?"

"I had a bad car accident about six years ago," she explained. "Put it through the windshield. I thought I would never be able to work again."

"Why?"

"The doctor flitted through my room after the surgery, and I thought he said, 'You'll *never* be able to use your hand again.'"

"He was wrong!" I exclaimed.

"No," Pam corrected me. "He didn't know I had a hearing problem, and I didn't understand his muttering. He actually said, 'You'll be able to use your hand.'"

"So how long before you got that cleared up?" I asked, referring to the misunderstanding.

"Couple of days," she admitted with a sheepish grin. "Of course, I was only thirty-four at the time. Life begins at thirty-five—just like Helen Trent."

Tragedy upon tragedy, I thought—the human condition. But Pam was again confirming my belief in the adaptability of the human spirit to overcome disappointment and diffculty. Life, after all, is more than just a string of successive advances toward inevitable dependence and death.

"You're thirty-five?" I finally asked incredulously.

"No," Pam admitted. "I'll be forty in August."

"I'm forty!" I declared. "My birthday was yesterday. Here's to forty." I raised my water glass to touch her coffee cup and glanced at my watch. It was 11:00, and the Cobblestone was closing.

Outside the entrance, we again shook hands, and I said I would call. She turned and walked to her car. The measured but uneven clack-clack-clack of her low-heeled shoes echoed off the pavement in the darkness. With the methodical clank-clank-clank of my crutches, I manuevered myself to my car door.

I had just met a survivor who, like me, was searching out those significant stepping stones that lead across difficulties to new understanding.

A year and a half later, on a rainy October, 1984 evening, we would exchange, by candlelight, these vows before three hundred friends and relatives:

We take each other as husband and wife as long as we both shall live. In our spiritual journey together, we pledge to share our lives openly with one another, to speak the truth to each other in love and challenge each other in our search for truth. We promise to honor and tenderly care for each other, to cherish and encourage each other's growth as individuals. We promise to love each other in the light of God's unending love in Christ.

Not-So-Quiet Desperation

Teach me to feel another's woe,
    To hide the fault I see;
That mercy I to others show,
    That mercy show to me.

—Alexander Pope
The Universal Prayer

It poured like wine. It looked like wine. And it stained the sleeve of my suit coat like wine. But it was my first communion in a Methodist church, and, even though I knew better, I was not prepared for the surprise I felt when I tasted it. It turned out to be grape juice.

To my Lutheran taste buds, it was like taking the first bite out of a Mounds candy bar, missing the mark and chomping, instead, on the cardboard insert below the bar.

I choked back an involuntary snicker at my surprise, pretending to have a slight cough which I politely covered by placing the bent forefinger of my right hand against my mouth.

But Pam, my fiancee, was sitting next to me. She caught my eye, and we both knew we were on the verge of slipping down a spiral of illogical thought that could result in an outright burst of rude laughter—a vulnerability I always need to guard against as a person without fine-tuned control over involuntary responses.

I tried logic to get out of my laughing mode. After all, this was her church. I didn't know communion was going to be served at the pew, and there was no convenient way not to participate—an option I usually chose in visiting a church for the first time.

Pam had just rescued me by grabbing my individual chalice and holding it for me as the usher served it. She knew it was too small for me to handle, but she had not yet perfected the grace it takes to help me sip from a tiny chalice. In the process, half the juice did not make it to my mouth and ended up, instead, on my sleeve.

Trying to hide the stain with my hand, I looked at Pam again as she was sipping her grape juice. She swallowed it quickly in desperation but then, in trying to cover up the inappropriate grin on her face, let out a snort.

I started to snicker again, and, in trying to hold it inside, lapsed into a deep heaving that moved my whole body. I threatened to burst into an uproarious laughter. Pressing my back against the pew, I bowed my head and forced myself to picture my mother's funeral. My face turned hot, and my armpits were damp.

Pam, trying to hide her grin, was employing another, perhaps wiser tactic. She was letting out short bursts of giggle—a giggle here, a giggle there—mixed strategically with the deeper notes of the solemn organ music.

That was the real problem. I had not yet learned how to let my silliness out gradually. Instead, the pressure was building, and I kept hearing myself repeatedly ask, "Are you laughing with us, Lord?"

Suddenly, I burst into a spurt of full laughter during the quietest of interludes. I finally muffled it by biting hard enough on my tongue to refocus my attention on the pain of reality instead of such derelict musings.

The couple sitting next to me—he in his navy blue suit and silver-gray hair, she in her aqua shirtdress and honey-blonde perm—looked gravely at both of us and then pretended to ignore us.

I tried to imagine myself small—so small that the parishioners around me couldn't see me because I was sitting under the pew. But that didn't help.

I felt like an idiot because everyone around me could see I was an idiot. And, deep in my brain, I knew I was going to hell for disturbing this most solemn of sacraments of the church.

Maybe idiots don't go to hell because they don't know any better. Maybe I should pretend I don't comprehend the travesty I had just committed as I walk out the church door. I'm a stranger in this congregation. No one knows me. And as an idiot, people would naturally ignore me. And I would be forgiven.

But that would be hypocrisy of the highest order and clearly mark me as a condemned person. It would also border on schizophrenia and put me on the path to sixteen sessions with a psychotherapist.

The congregation stood, and as I did likewise, I stiffly looked around me. No one was looking at me. I swiped a glance into the vacant faces of the couple next to me. I imagined what it would be like to be at peace with one's self. They looked so calm and collected. It was as if they had truly received absolution.

Had they left their inner thoughts conveniently at the door as they entered the sanctuary? Or did they also have their own chronic vulnerabilities, their innate weaknesses, their twisted rationales? Perhaps I just couldn't see them.

The service finally ended, and, as the parishioners around us slowly filtered out of the pews, Pam and I stood there at our seats. Pam nestled her face into my shoulder.

“That was awful,” she finally said, her voice muffled by my suit lapel. She giggled again but stopped short. I looked into her eyes and saw disappointment. “I shouldn’t have looked at you. I just couldn’t help myself.”

“I know, honey,” I said, limp with exhaustion but buoyed by relief. I hugged her, realizing how much we needed each other’s love, understanding, and forgiveness.

A Jump Start for Both of Us

Throw out the lifeline across the dark wave,
There is a brother whom someone should save.

—Edward Smith Ufford
Throw Out the Lifeline

I was running low on gas and still fifty miles from home on this dark, cold November afternoon in 1993. I didn't want to stop to gas up because I was listening to an important University of Wisconsin-Ohio State football game on my car radio and wanted to get home to watch it on TV with Pam.

Besides, I dread self-service gas stations—largely because they are not *service* stations anymore. Full-service stations are a rarity nowadays, and I have the location of every one of them along my frequently traveled routes mapped out in my mind.

But filling my car with gas is no big deal. I do it all the time.

So I pulled off the freeway, deciding to stop at a new Amoco station which took credit cards at the pump.

How convenient, I thought. Paying at the pump will at least save me time (getting my crutches out of the car, walking to the store's counter, fiddling in my pants pocket to find my billfold, etc.).

At the pump I turned off the car but left my radio on and the car door open, forgetting my headlights were on. I would listen to the game while taking only a few minutes to fill my tank.

I know I'm not a whiz when it comes to technology, so I carefully read the instructions on the pump, popped the most common credit card I had into the machine, and watched for instructions. Card not valid, it replied. A second and a third try yielded the same results.

Ohio State was on Wisconsin's 10-yard line.

I finally pushed, "Pay Inside," filled my gas tank and hopped back into the car to drive up to the convenience store's front door.

My car wouldn't start.

It was then that I realized that I had left my headlights on. I turned both the lights and radio off and tried again. Nothing. Was the battery that weak? I had just had my 1990 Maxima winterized the day before.

I sat there for a minute, thinking it would turn over after a little bit of rest. No. It was dead.

The people inside the store were watching. I could feel it. I could imagine what they were saying inside the store. Something like, "The guy doesn't have a brain in his head."

Suddenly, a woman in a ragged coat popped out of the store, swept up to my window, grabbed my credit card, and ran back to the store.

When she returned with my receipt, she realized I had worn the battery down even more. "Just stay in the car," she said, the cold wind blowing her hair. "I'll jump ya."

She ran to what I assumed was her personal car (a rusty vintage-70's Pontiac), parked it nose-to-nose with my car, and placed her jumper cables on my terminals. I tried to start my car again. Nothing.

She ran back to the store, and I began looking for my AAA card and to see how much cash I had.

Suddenly, she was back. She switched the jumper cables on my terminals, I turned the key on my ignition, and my car started.

I handed her a ten-dollar bill with a "thank you." My words seemed hollow. She wouldn't take the money at first, but I insisted.

Another motorist in the next lane, who apparently had watched the whole episode while she was gassing up, probably summed it up better. "That's service," she cheerfully commented to us both.

We all need experiences that validate what is good about us, but we don't always get them or recognize them in our daily rush.

I'm sometimes desperate—in real need of help, and many times there is that special someone who takes a few minutes to truly help me.

As our paths cross, we provide a jump start for each other and then go our separate ways—renewed with the spark of what it is to be human. We leave each other with a feeling of completeness we all long for but seldom replicate on a daily basis.

Those jump starts often stick with us throughout a lifetime and recharge us every time we remember them.

New Patterns, Old Habits

Everyone complains of his memory, and no one complains of his judgement.

—Francois Duc De La Rochefoucauld
Reflections

I need to do a better job of anticipating what lane I want to be in.

I was running late in my drive home from Milwaukee, but I wanted to pick up a book, *Life After Television*, I had reserved at the University Book Store in Madison.

"Fascinating book," a friend had told me. "The personal computer is going to change completely how we receive information and give us a truly interactive medium. Network TV is going to be less of an influence on our lives during the next ten years—great opportunity for those who know how to take advantage of these changes."

I hit most of the stoplights going down East Washington Avenue just right, but then a brief but intense shower slowed the traffic as I approached downtown Madison.

As I turned onto East Johnson, I was thinking about the link between TV and computers and taking my normal route home. But then I realized I was in the wrong lane for my Lake Street turnoff and the University Book Store. So I gradually inched my way across three lanes of traffic—taking chances and trusting the good will of strangers—in a stop-and-go pattern that covered three blocks.

I pulled into the parking lot behind the University Book Store and decided to use my worn crutches instead of my Amigo electric scooter to run into the store to get the book.

Splashing through pools of water standing in the alley behind the store, I approached the front entrance just in time to take advantage of an offer from a student to hold the door open as I scooted into the familiar entryway of drab concrete. Third floor, I told myself, and approached the elevator.

Before I could punch the elevator button, the man in the information booth behind me said, "Sorry, the elevator is temporarily out of order. They're fixing it now. You hit us at the wrong time."

"No problem," I said without acknowledging him with direct eye contact. I looked up at the three short flights of stairs and grabbed the left railing, leaving my left Canadian crutch dangle as I used the right crutch as support to walk quite easily up the stairs.

It wasn't until I almost got to the third floor that I noticed the store had remodeled its general books section with new tile, which had sweeping swirls of mint, beige, and raspberry.

Pleasing but safe pastels, I thought. I poked both of my crutches onto the shiny floor ahead of me for support. Instead of gaining enough support to pull myself upright and proceed in a walking position, I suddenly found myself plunging both crutches ahead of me in several quick jabs, desperately attempting to gain some footing (or more accurately *crutching*).

But the crutch tips were worn smooth—and wet—and the new floor was waxed to perfection for easy cleaning.

Both crutches slid beyond my reach and hit the floor with a clatter. Still crouched from the last step of the stairs, my full weight sank to my right knee and the knuckles on both my hands.

Under my breath, I cussed the rain, I cussed the wet, worn crutch tips (which never grip when wet), and I cussed the pastel tile. And I cussed the out-of-order elevator.

The commotion in the newly tiled entry startled the woman at the checkout counter nearby, and I could hear her call. "Charlie . . . Charlie."

I quickly checked my knuckles. They were OK. No blood. I flexed my knee. OK.

Apparently, Charlie (of some authority) had heard the racket, too, for he was right there. "Are you all right? Can I help you up?" I could hear both real personal concern and the liability question in his voice.

"I'm OK," I said, as I started crawling to the nearest wall so I could pull myself up and retrieve my crutches.

"Can I help you?" Charlie again asked. "Are you all right?"

By that time, I was up, and he could see I did not injure myself.

"Can we help you find what you need?" asked the woman at the check-out counter.

"No, that's fine," I declined. "I need to go back there." I pointed to the back of the store.

"When you check out, I'll call one of the guys to take you down on the service elevator," she suggested.

"Fine," I replied, knowing that I needed to get home and that even a service elevator would be faster than going down three flights of stairs.

I proceeded to the back of the store, where I had picked up my reserved books before, but, after three rows of bookshelves, I didn't know where to go. The large wrap-around service desk which had always been there was gone.

"Where's the service desk?" I finally asked another clerk sitting at a lone computer in an open area at aisle five.

Reserved books were apparently not her area, but she got the book for me as I waited at her terminal and watched her retrace my steps back to the check-out lines. I then saw the new service desk just to the left of the entrance.

After she came back with my book, I returned to the check-out line, taking the same route she had just taken.

At the check-out line, I waited for a man in shipping to come out and take me down the service elevator. Of course, the service elevator was in back of the store, and the shipping clerk kindly walked with me as I cautiously negotiated the slippery floors across the width of the store for a third time.

As we took the lumbering elevator in the back of the store down to shipping and receiving's ground level, I berated myself for not taking advantage of the first offer of help from the woman at the check-out. Charlie could have saved me some time and effort by going to the service desk and getting my book for me. And how could I expect to snap back into a normal pattern and walk through the store anonymously after making such an unusual entrance?

We finally got down to ground level, but that also presented a new challenge—at least in the mind of the shipping clerk. The shipping dock had three steps down to the sidewalk of the alley.

"I can make those," I assured the shipping clerk, but apparently he had received his orders from third floor. He removed a huge box from an adjacent lift, helped me step gently onto the lift's jiggling, open platform and slowly lowered me three feet to the ground.

How Does
Obtaining Balance
Apply to Your Situation?

1. What experiences have helped you form your perception of human nature?

2. Under what circumstances do you decide asking for help is better than trying to cope with a situation all by yourself?

3. In what ways do you find and draw upon the strengths of other *escapees* from expectation?

4. What do you do to reconcile the difference between perception and reality in awkward situations?

5. How do you repay a person who unexpectedly helps you out of a helpless situation?

6. In what cases do you benefit by learning to adjust to a new set of circumstances?

Chapter 7

Discovering Happiness

Detours

Life is the garment we continually alter,
but which never seems to fit.

—David McCord
Whereas to Mr. Franklin

Being there was the most important aspect of my life at that time.

Even though I was on a new campus in a new dorm ready to meet my new roommate, Phil, I felt I belonged.

I had already moved in and had looked at Phil's name on the front of the door, trying to imagine how to pronounce Streichen, his last name.

Phil first entered our assigned dorm room as I sat on the edge of my bed on the side of the room I had chosen. He carefully placed a large suitcase, an ROTC uniform, and black boots beside the bed opposite mine.

He turned to shake my hand, and I stood to meet a tall, straight, fit man with blue eyes and a crew cut of red hair. In response, I felt myself trying to stand straighter, but he still towered over me. He had a confident handshake.

"Hi, I'm Phil," he said stiffly. "You're Jim, right?"

He didn't wait for an answer.

"There must be some mistake here," he said calmly.

"Last spring, I and my buddy made arrangements to room together this year."

I saw him glance at my Canadian crutches, which I had propped in the corner of my open closet.

"Let me check with the housefellow," Phil was saying. "I'll be back."

He shut the door behind him, and I sat there, wondering what to do with a roommate who did not want to be my roommate.

I had met our housefellow, Pete, the day before. A pipe smoker, Pete looked older than most of the guys on the floor. A psychology major, he was tough-looking and had a serious side about him that only occasionally broke into a faint grin.

How did they pair up roommates anyway? Was it the luck of the draw? Or did someone put some thought into the process?

It was 1963, and fall classes were about to begin at the University of Wisconsin-Madison campus. As a junior, I was a transfer student from Platteville State, a much smaller campus in the southwestern corner of Wisconsin.

Three years earlier, I was denied admission to the Madison campus—not because of my SAT scores or high school grades but because the university had very few students with disabilities on campus at that time. It was not equipped to handle people with special needs.

The people at the admissions office could not see how I could get from class to class on the hilly Madison campus—especially with only fifteen minutes between classes.

So I took a detour and for two years attended Platteville, temporarily putting aside my dream of graduating from the University of Wisconsin-Madison—a vision that had driven me since seventh grade.

Platteville was a former teachers college on flat terrain where all of my classes were in Old Main. Only two "B's" (both in Spanish) during the last two years had prevented me from being a straight "A" student.

Still, friends had questioned why I was transferring to the Madison campus, which had a reputation for being tougher academically.

I knew I could do it, but I needed to be focused. My goal was to graduate in two years and get the highest grades I could so I could get a job as a copywriter in a Chicago advertising agency, be self-supporting, marry, and have a home of my own.

I had purchased a pair of Canadian crutches the spring before my transfer to Madison and learned how to walk with them. Each day that summer, I would walk as fast as I could from our farm house in the valley to the edge of the woods at the top of the hill, overlooking our dairy farm.

By fall, I could make it to the top of the hill and back in fifteen minutes.

I was ready for the Madison campus.

But was Phil ready for me?

Phil opened the door, bringing in another suitcase, which he placed beside the bed.

"I can move," I found myself saying in forced speech that I'm sure was difficult for Phil to understand. "If you've made other arrangements, I can find another roommate."

"No, that's not necessary," he said, starting to unpack.

Pause.

"I have cerebral palsy," I admitted. "If you don't understand me, just say so."

"I know. I know what it is," he said. "My cousin's daughter has it. She's five. They live in Sauk City."

"I grew up on a dairy farm not far from there—near Loganville."

"Really? I always liked the farm. I'm from Milwaukee, but I've spent summers on my uncle's farm in Vernon County. I'd like to have a farmette someday—after I retire from the Army."

Pause.

"You sure you don't want to switch roommates?" I had to ask it again.

"No," Phil said again. "My buddy's just down the hall. Besides, I don't know how long he'll be here. Mike and I are in ROTC together. He's worried things in Vietnam are going to clear up before he graduates and gets his chance for a tour of duty over there. He's talking about quitting school after this first semester."

Phil placed his ROTC boots in the far corner of his open closet.

"Let's see . . . ," he said softly, almost to himself, as he hung up his uniform. "Let's see how things work out."

Crossing the Red Line

And indeed there will be time to wonder, 'Do I dare?' and, 'Do I dare?'

—T. S. Eliot

The Love Song of J. Alfred Prufrock

It was a narrow, wooden bridge, just broad enough for one vehicle to cross the Zambezi River between Zambia and Rhodesia. I gingerly placed each foot and each crutch on one plank at a time, trying to avoid the one-inch gaps between them. In the hot, oppressive humidity of the rain forest, the rubber handlegrips on my crutches became greasy under my wet palms.

I stopped to catch my breath in the thick air and look over the bridge's railing. About thirty feet below, the water churned as it hit the first rocks which led to Victoria Falls on my right. But, to my disappointment, I couldn't see the falls. All I could see—and feel—was a heavy mist that blocked out the western horizon and the hot afternoon sun.

I continued to inch toward the center of the bridge with the other members of our People-to-People delegation, and then I saw it—just as Lila, our guide, had described it to us earlier that day. A red stripe, two planks wide, ran across the full width of the bridge.

"This is where we have to stop," Lila, in a tan cotton dress, reminded us in her British accent. "Zambia and Rhodesia are officially at war with each other, and we can't take any chances. For the last six months we periodically have had raids back and forth across the border."

The thick jungle on the opposite side of the river was hazy, mysterious, but peaceful. Below the bridge a small excursion boat for tourists blew a warning whistle as it passed two men in a fishing boat.

"Next we'll take a boat ride on the river," said Lila, a tall, thin woman who had crowned her head of long blonde hair with a blue cap, a masculine accessory which seemed odd for a woman to wear in 1973. "Then we'll go down below the falls. You may be able to see some hippos in the water up here, but it's hard. Their backs look like smooth rocks in the water. They'll be easier to see from the boat."

Numbed by the stifling humidity, many of the twenty-five Wisconsinites in our group, dressed in sticky polyester casuals, hung to the railings and searched the waters anyway for a hippo.

I was more interested in the red line. I took a couple of steps back from the group and quietly placed the tip of my left crutch over the red line and then pulled it back. No gunfire. No screaming warriors hit the bridge from Zambia's side. No military men showed up. But Lila caught me out of the corner of her eye and smiled.

"It's time to go," she suggested to me, hinting I should get a head start on the others in our retreat from the bridge.

At least my crutch had been on Zambia's side of the bridge. I imagined the possibilities of an ambush that I would encounter by walking through the rain forest across the river.

Before retracing my steps back to the bus, I again looked at the red line, amused that human beings throughout the world recognize it as a command to stop and proceed no further.

It reminded me of the day, twenty-one years before, when I first encountered this universal mark for dividing people. For the first time during my third year at Washington Orthopedic School in Madison, I had gotten to the gym before Mr. Quinn, our gym teacher, and the other third and fourth graders.

The far wall looked different as my feet hit the polished, hardwood floor. Someone had left the door open between the orthopedic gym and the regular gym. I skated my stiff feet across the salmon-colored floor. I stopped amid the red and green stripes of the basketball court, fighting for balance and gasping for air in my excitement.

I looked back. No one was coming from the orthopedic wing of the school. Through the doorway I heard a gym teacher's whistle blow, but I continued to shuffle across the floor.

As I reached the open door, I quickly peeked in and saw two students sallying up thick ropes which hung from the ceiling. The instructor and his class of older boys, all in gym clothes, formed a circle around the two classmates climbing the ropes.

I again looked back. No one. I instinctively knew the thick red line on the gym floor between the two doorjambs meant the much larger, unfamiliar gym beyond the doorway was forbidden territory for anyone with a brace, crutch, wheelchair, or (in my case) spastic condition. But I stepped across it to get a better view of the action on the ropes.

Just then someone grabbed my shoulder. I jumped. It was Mr. Quinn.

"This is not our gym, Jimmy," he said calmly. "It's time for our class."

He followed me across the red line as I stepped back through the doorway. But I caught one last glimpse of the guys on the ropes before he closed the door with a thud.

The thud echoed off the walls of yellow concrete block above the racket of bouncing basketballs, squeaking wheelchair tires, clanking leg braces, and delighted squeals. We were a ragtag group dressed in stiff corduroys, flannel shirts, and drab cardigans.

We knew firsthand about polio, cerebral palsy, spinal bifida, mental retardation, seizures, and muscular dystrophy. But we didn't know about rope climbing.

As we formed a circle to bounce the basketball between partners within our group, I looked up at the ceiling and imagined how frightening it would be to climb a rope to even the lowest girder.

Slipping through the Clutches of Ketchum, Tobias & Yael

Every bed we make in life, based on personal presupposition, becomes narrow upon our first turn beneath its covers.

—Anonymous

"What a great shade of red!" I remarked to Yael in a string of mashed consonants as nine-year-old Andrea again skipped into the living room.

"Pardon?" Yael asked quietly with a puzzled look. She was sitting across from me in a caramel rocker. I patted the right arm of the red, gold, and beige sofa on which I was sitting. Andrea stood silently next to her mom, eyeing my crutches, which I had placed on the chocolate carpet in front of the dazzling couch.

"I like this hint of red in your couch," I clarified, choosing a combination of words I thought Yael—and Andrea—would probably better understand. I had just met Andrea for the first time. "Great job of decorating."

"Oh, I thought you said, 'Want to go to bed?'" Yael interrupted with an earnest look on her face.

I saw her eyes twinkle beneath her dark hair, which was peppered with gray. Her flush face broke into a broad smile.

"No-o-o . . ." I finally replied in disbelief that my comment could be so misunderstood. "I said I like this red." I felt a nervous smirk cross my face, as I patted the couch's cushion next to me.

Yael's petite giggle exploded into throaty laughter.

Andrea watched me with wide eyes as she nervously curled her long black hair between the thumb and forefinger of her right hand. How could a mom be so open about our misunderstanding in front of her nine-year-old daughter? How could our communication get so off track? We had only known each other a couple of months. Was she thinking, all along, what it would be like to sleep with a man who has cerebral palsy? Or was it just my sloppy speech?

"When did you do all this?" I asked, deciding to ignore the misunderstanding and expand on my original comment. I couldn't recall the room's colors from my first visit.

"A couple of weeks ago . . . "

"Jamie wants me to come over and play with her trains," Andrea finally piped up.

"Fine," Yael approved, and Andrea skipped to the front door. "Back in a half hour?"

"Yeah," Andrea answered from the hallway.

"Our neighbor's daughter is into model railroading."

"Well, that's refreshing," I said with a chuckle. "I usually associate scaled-down trains with sixty-year-old men."

We didn't fit the norm as a couple either. Perhaps that's why we were attracted to each other. Yael was Jewish, a single mother of two daughters. She was able-bodied and carefree. I was single, never married, a German Lutheran, disabled, and uptight.

We were both writers and called public relations our profession, and that's how we met. She worked at the public relations agency I had chosen as outside support for my communication department at a soon-to-be Fortune 500 company. But that was not our common bond.

Rather, we both felt a basic need to go beyond conventional expectations and deal with reality on our own terms.

"Why do you spend time with a cripple?" Yael's mother had asked her. It was a revelation for Yael that she shared with me during our last date—a discovery we perhaps all have to face at some point in our lives that we have grown beyond the perceptions of our parents. The same people who taught us the alphabet at four reflect, years later, an earlier generation's norms that may not mesh with what we think is today's reality.

"She's out of it," Yael lamented at the time.

"Maybe not," I assured her. "A family's skeletons are always best left in the closet."

"Skeletons?"

"I mean members of the family who happen to be eccentric . . . disabled . . . gay . . . elderly . . . unattractive," I rattled off. "We all have skeletons. They hurt a family's image as fine breeding stock when the younger generation goes out 'courtin'."

A tiny giggle again escaped from Yael's throat.

Deep down I think we both knew that some of the social norms of the 1950s were still alive in 1981. I was surprised to discover that Yael's mother was more concerned about my physical condition than my non-Jewish heritage. Somehow I expected urban people to be more contemporary in their attitudes than those I had grown up with in rural America.

After that second house visit, Yael and I gradually drifted apart, although we kept in touch. Six months later, she called me and mentioned she was writing to an extraordinary man, Toby, who was in prison. They wrote every day, she said.

"Extraordinary?" I asked with a laugh.

"He's a lawyer and a fantastic writer," she said seriously. "He's got such a sense of humor."

At the time I didn't ask why he was in prison. But I was surprised to learn the next time I talked to her that Yael and Toby were planning to get married.

"Come visit us," Yael suggested over the phone. "I've told Toby all about you. I quit my job. Toby can't practice law anymore, but we've formed our own advertising business here at home. It may be something you'll want to consider. We could do almost anything for you. Toby has so many connections. He's brilliant. We're calling ourselves Ketchum, Tobias and Yael. Isn't that classy?"

"That's class," I agreed, trying to show a little more enthusiasm than I was feeling at the moment.

We did meet. And Yael was right. Toby was tall, dark, handsome, and brilliant. He had outfitted their basement with a computer, a copier, and a light table.

"As you can see, we've got the setup—and the brilliance—to do an extraordinary job for you," Toby pitched, as he threw his arm around Yael.

"I can see that," I replied, using a quick glance around the basement offices as an excuse not to look at Yael.

"You have a masters?" Toby asked as he climbed the basement steps behind me, presenting himself as an awkward human shield against the fall he expected me to take at any moment.

"No," I said meekly.

"Should take a look at it," he urged. "May help in your circumstances."

I went home, amused by how rapidly a person's circumstances can change. Two days later I received a call from Yael, again asking for my business. In reply, I wrote a business letter, addressed to both of them, explaining in concrete terms why I thought Ketchum Tobias & Yael was not the right fit for my company's needs.

I never heard from Yael or Toby again.

Risky Business

I celebrate myself and sing myself,
and what I assume you shall assume.

—Walt Whitman
Leaves of Grass

With the grip of my black briefcase spindled onto my right crutch handle, I stepped into the elevator, dragging my feet into the cubicle already occupied by two men, who leaned against opposite walls.

I punched the button for the twelfth floor and waited for the door to close, feeling a brief sense of relief that I had once again passed through an elevator door, over which I had no control, before it closed on me.

We quickly surveyed one another with our eyes and then watched the first floor light go out as we began our trip together up one of the Radisson towers in Minneapolis.

Not conventioneers, I thought, as I caught the younger of the two men eyeing the lapel of my suit.

"Vice president," he suddenly said, almost to himself.

At first, I didn't know what he was talking about, but I then followed his eye to my lapel and remembered that I still had my name badge on. It had been a long day.

"That's something," he said a bit louder. "*I'm* not even a vice president."

I smiled at the guy out of disbelief but didn't say anything. What a narcissist, I told myself. I tried to ignore him by watching the other man rock back on his heels and stare at the control buttons until the elevator finally stopped at the twelfth.

The door opened, and I scooted myself out of the elevator just in time before the door again closed.

The '80s were go-go years for business—when Ivan Boesky, an MBA, and the California economy were hot. And being a vice president of any organization—no matter how small, insignificant, or financially insecure—was in.

At least, that's what I told myself as I returned to my room. But the elevator incident kept popping up in my mind now and then, and I didn't know why. Years later a friend, Pat, a reporter for *The Capital Times,* clarified it for me during one of our occasional lunches together at Crandall's.

"Because you've succeeded in overcoming great difficulties and accomplished things that some of us have not, you remind us of the potential we're not using," Pat said. He was a balding, slight man whose rimless glasses glinted as he spoke.

"That's the last thing I want to do," I replied, shaking my head. "Make someone feel guilty—that's definitely not my intent."

"It's not always guilt," he said quickly, taking another sip of coffee. "Your example can be turned into a positive experience."

"Yeah," I said, basking in Pat's understanding. "That's what I would prefer."

"But some people who are struggling with self-esteem can allow their 'self talk' to use your example as a reproach," Pat explained. "Your circumstances force a person to confront his own self-image. Does he feel good about himself?

Or does he know, deep down, that he's not applying himself like he could—that maybe he doesn't have the skills he needs, he doesn't know the tricks of the trade . . . "

He asked the waitress for more coffee, and I continued to sip my Coke.

"I still believe most people are just surprised to see a guy with crutches carrying a briefcase with a title of V-P," I added.

"That, too," Pat agreed, almost in a whisper. "You don't fit the stereotype. You surprise people, and that means they have to readjust their image of what people with disabilities are all about."

"That's probably what happens first," I said, thinking through a predicament I hadn't discussed with anyone else before. "They're surprised and maybe uncomfortable because they have to readjust their stereotype about people with disabilities. Then they internalize it—for better or worse."

"And you have no control over how people are going to internalize it," Pat pointed out. "Each person handles it a little bit differently."

"They have no control over such circumstances either," I said sheepishly, "because they never know when they'll meet someone like me in an elevator and have to deal with it."

Trapped by Shriveled Imagination

To know is nothing at all; to imagine is everything.

—Anatole France
The Crime of Sylvestre Bonnard

It was another interview about why I was different, and it started out with the commonplace question: "So, how do you describe your condition?"

"I have cerebral palsy," I answered automatically.

"And how long have you had this?" Bonita again asked in a mellow South African accent. Under apartheid in South Africa, she was classified as "colored," neither black or white. But she had lived in Germany, which explained why her soft voice sometimes uncharacteristically broke into harsh guttural sounds. She was softly flamboyant and dangerously "different." Her quiet brashness was sometimes unsettling in the everyday routine of our small town in Wisconsin.

"Since birth," I replied casually. "My mother couldn't have a normal delivery, but her doctor didn't realize it until it was too late. He performed a C-section at the last minute."

"Why couldn't she have a natural delivery?" Bonita rapidly fired back. She was a plump woman of thirty-five who wore a full, ankle-length skirt of orange, yellow, and red that flounced out to cover both arms of one of the four chairs around our oak dinette set.

"My mother had rickets as a child, so she had a deformed pelvis," I answered.

At fifty, I had fielded the same questions time after time as a part of who I was and why I was different. People needed to know.

Besides, Bonita was our neighbor, and she had called a week before to say she needed an interview with Pam and me for her social work course. And I savored the thought that I had a story to tell that piqued the interest of a woman who had lived in three different cultures.

But I saw Pam, who sat across from me, roll her eyes in disbelief.

"So what happened?" Bonita asked in a soft, throaty voice, as she looked up from her note pad. Her black hair, short and wavy, glistened under the light of the chandelier above our table.

"The doctor didn't check things out until it was too late. The brain injury had already occurred," I curtly explained. "Our family minister finally called for a spinal tap. That's what saved me. It released the pressure on my brain and prevented further damage."

Pam squirmed in her chair. It then occurred to me that, even though we had been married eight years, she had not heard me tell someone else the complete story of why I walked and talked with difficulty.

"Tell me about how you went to school," Bonita coaxed. "I know nowadays we have what we call 'mainstreaming.' " Her brown elastic face broke into a grin, revealing two deep dimples on each side of her small mouth.

Pam thoughtfully traced the contours of her chin with her right hand.

"Well, I tried to go to first grade at our one-room school house, which was one mile from our farm," I enthusiastically began. We had finally progressed beyond the preliminary explanations to what, for me, was the real purpose of the interview.

"I didn't make it through first grade," I continued. "The teacher was not trained to handle kids with special needs. So, my mother taught me first grade at home, and then I went to a special orthopedic school in Madison for kids with disabilities."

"What about high school?"

"I went back home to our regular high school," I explained.

"So now you're a successful businessman with a nice new house," Bonita gushed.

"Well—yes . . . " I finally agreed, uncomfortable with the patronizing adjectives she was using.

Many people are successful in business. Many people have nice homes. I was probably biased, but, yes—I thought we had built our home with a consistent vision of its form and function, unlike her monstrosity which was a hodgepodge of European and American design.

At any rate, she had just skipped three decades of my life as an adult. Maybe that's why Bonita's home sat half-built and vacant for six months of "builder-owner" debate, and she ended up with a two-car garage that could house a basketball court. Perhaps her builder, thinking linear, couldn't span the gulf between what she liked in both design approaches and what could be shaped into a logical floor plan.

"I also wanted to ask you two about your marriage," Bonita suddenly stated. "When were you married?"

"1984," Pam offered without blinking.

I quickly recalled my story about how Pam and I had met in anticipation of her next question.

"You don't have to talk about this, if you don't want to," Bonita said quickly. Her brown eyes grew larger. "I was just wondering how you find your sexual relationship?"

"What do you mean?" Pam asked with a puzzled smirk on her face.

"I mean have you had to make any adjustments?" Bonita continued, searching for the clinically approved words.

"Not really," I chimed in, trying to imagine the *adjustments* Bonita had in mind. With a mixture of amusement, anger, and disappointment, I looked at Pam, who was pursing her lips to hide an exploding grin.

"I know Harold and I have been together four years, and we're still learning," Bonita admitted with a giggle. "I'm usually all set to go, you know, but it takes Harold time, and I've had to learn how to help him get ready."

Silence.

Pam's eyes narrowed. Her grin had disappeared.

I tried to image the various ways Bonita could help Harold get ready and wanted to ask her about those particular adjustments, but I didn't.

"So, would you call your sexual relationship normal?"

"Normal," I agreed with a gulp, not sure what *normal* meant.

Pam stifled another grin and nodded.

"Normal," she repeated.

Uncommon Bond

I am a parcel of vain strivings tied together
by a chance bond.

—Henry David Thoreau
Sic Vita

He ran up to me with a shrill scream and grabbed my hair with both fists. His screeching stopped, but he clenched both fists of my hair tightly against the top of my head.

It was one of the most demeaning acts anyone could perpetrate on me, for my hair—thick and black—is important to my self-image. After shampooing it each morning, I let it dry naturally and then meticulously brush and spray it so it will stay in place throughout the day.

But he was mangling that morning's creation in an abrupt halt to our long-range planning committee's quick tour of Silver Springs Elementary School. Was there no respect for prim leaders of the community among today's grade school students?

He hovered over me as I sat still in my Amigo electric scooter. He had invaded my space and put me in an awkward, embarrassing situation. I could feel the resolve in his fingers. He was not going to let go of my hair.

Without moving my head, I glanced up at the school principal, a slender, shy woman who stood next to the classroom door in pathetic shock. After all, she was in charge. She had been guiding our long-range planning committee through each classroom of the school, a new facility that was the gem of the school district. We were evaluating the district's school facilities.

His fists relaxed, and I slowly hunched over the handlebar of my scooter, trying to protect myself. But then he grabbed a tighter grip. The watch on my wrist, now not more than two inches from my face, ticked off long seconds—five . . . six . . . seven . . .

Why did he have to pick me as his bonding partner in front of this group? I was trying to prove myself to the superintendent of schools—and the committee. True, I had no background in education, but I knew the elements of a strategic planning process. Although I could not speak fast enough or plain enough to keep up with the more vocal members of the committee, I at least had a normal intelligence.

But I was out of touch. After all, I had not been inside a school for twenty-five years. Since when do high schools have patrol people in the hallways? Why do you have to pass through a scanner as you come out of the school library? And I didn't know about the TMR (Trainable Mentally Retarded) classes.

15 . . . 16 . . . 17 . . . my watch ticked on. I kept waiting for his teacher to help me out of this predicament, but I didn't know where she was. I had been the last one of our group to enter the TMR room. We were interrupting her class time, but the principal had invited our group into the room.

I had planned just to peek in from the doorway, but the principal motioned for me to enter. So I switched my electric scooter into forward and went in. It was then that I suddenly found myself locked into this hair-wrenching experience with one of the students.

As he continued to pull my hair, a soft purr of delight came from his throat. Somehow I understood his delight. It was something I always wanted to do myself to the class brat we had in third grade. But at the time, I just didn't have the courage—or the sanity—to do it.

I glanced up at the district's superintendent of schools, who stood motionless and expressionless not more than ten feet away from me. No one knew what to do.

Finally, my *companion* let go of my hair, and his teacher promptly escorted him back to his desk. Our long-range planning committee, apparently not adept at adjusting to short-term situations, quickly followed me as I put my scooter into reverse and backed into the hallway.

"Quite a welcome," the superintendent of schools whispered to me after the principal silently closed the classroom door behind her. I giggled, feeling relieved to have escaped the situation without a hassle, and looked for further assurances from others on the committee. But no one else in our group offered a comment.

"That's Steve," the superintendent finally explained to the group as we walked down the hall, following the principal to the gym, the next stop on our tour. "He just joined the TMR class this week. He's still under observation."

Steering and controlling the speed of my scooter with my right hand to keep up with the group, I ran my left hand through my hair and felt two spikes, stiff with hair spray, sticking straight up on both sides of my head. I tried to rub them down with my palm, but they snapped right up again—a constant reminder of the incident.

As we entered the gym, I grabbed a comb from my pocket and tried to tame my two hair spikes, but the comb only made them floppy, like two rabbit ears. They popped up after each combing.

Were the other committee members being politically correct in their silence, quietly repeating to themselves the cliche, "Birds of a feather flock together?" I had spent years trying to assert myself as an individual who didn't necessarily have a bond with every other person who happened to have a disability. Just because I was left-handed, after all, didn't mean I would have a natural affinity for anyone else who was left-handed.

But why did I excite him? Why did he pick me? Was it my black suit or red tie? Was it my scooter? School kids, I noticed, are intrigued by a scooter driven by batteries.

Maybe it was because I was eye-level with him. Did the contortions in my face mirror his own?

Or is there some kind of universal, common bond we do not yet fully understand—a fundamental kinship we all have as human beings but rarely acknowledge or completely tap during our daily rituals with family, friends, and acquaintances?

How Does Discovering Happiness Apply to Your Situation?

1. What experiences reveal for you the potential—and the excitement—of trying new opportunities?

2. When is it beneficial for you to break away from convention?

3. What circumstances help you discover what you want out of life?

4. What responsibility are you willing to share in helping others understand your potential?

5. In what instances have you harnessed the power of imagination to make your life more fulfilling?

6. When have you felt the common bond of humanity, and how has that made your life richer?

Chapter 8

Savoring Satisfaction

Simple Suppositions

We dance round in a ring and suppose,
but the Secret sits in the middle and knows.

—Robert Frost
The Secret Sits

I knew she had discovered my secret crush when I saw, "Bye, Bye, Love," scribbled in spastic handwriting across her tan notebook. I caught a glimpse of it as she put the notebook in her book bag, but I just sat there in the desk behind her, pretending to be busy on my math.

I looked up at Ann as she stood to leave the room. Her blue eyes met mine for a split second, and her pout, made all the more obvious by the tight cheek muscles in her round face, sent a chill up my spine.

"What does that mean?" I asked, pointing to the scribbling on the tablet. She shrugged, looked me squarely in the face, and headed for the door, dragging her left foot slightly in a repeated shuffle that was wearing down the sole of her brown leather shoe's front toe.

Ann knew. I could tell by her clenched jaw and pursed lips. But why did she have to be so dramatic—and so creative—about it? "Bye, Bye Love." I had never seen it put that way before, but that about summed up my feelings.

Two kids in the eighth grade. Both with cerebral palsy. Both intelligent. Both determined to make it in life. It seemed everyone assumed we would someday make a good couple. And ever since sixth grade, I could tell Ann was beginning to make that assumption, too.

But it was not going to happen. Ann was bossy, judgmental, cunning, possessive—exactly what a thirteen-year-old boy didn't need. To be dominated by a short, pudgy woman at my age was a curse. She was rough and quick to ridicule with a frown between her distant eyes that dominated her round, Polish face.

Thelma, on the other hand, was smooth. She was tall, thin, graceful, charming. She had been a student at a regular school, and she would be with us for only half a year for physical therapy because she had a slight limp from polio. I was infatuated.

It didn't matter to her we were different. It didn't matter to us she was black. But the *Weekly Reader* contained words such as Selma and Montgomery and photos of black marchers and Southern riots.

Maybe that's why our teacher, Miss Singleton, a tall lady with graying hair, appeared worried about how we would react to Thelma's blackness. Maybe that's why Miss Singleton talked to all fifteen of us—all three grades—about differences before Thelma took the back desk in our row of five eighth graders.

I didn't know why Miss Singleton was talking about differences until Thelma showed up. It was her secret that Thelma was black, and she did not know how to tell us, except in her stern sermon about differences.

At first, I thought Gene or Kelly, two of the bigger sixth grade kids who had epilepsy, had again been caught shooting baskets outside in the playground that was reserved for the regular students of Washington Grade School.

That was not the problem. The problem was placing a black student into an all-white, upper-grade classroom against a backdrop of turmoil in the South.

When Thelma joined us that first day, there was no problem. After all, we were a group of kids with retardation, muscular dystrophy, polio, cerebral palsy, spinal bifida, seizures, and assorted bone and skin diseases among us. Who could be more different than we were?

Thelma looked me straight in the eye the first time I met her. She didn't stare at my strangely bent arms and legs. She didn't cringe at my sloppy speech.

Thelma was not like the white kids from the regular section of our school. Whenever they would accidentally run into one of us in the parking lot or the playground, they would often stare at us and maybe giggle or laugh and whisper to their friends about us.

Back in fourth grade, Orlando, a gangly, grinning black kid with polio, was my buddy. No one prepared me for Orlando. No one prepared Orlando for me. We just became buddies. But that was in 1952, when Ike, not Martin Luther King or George Wallace, was making the headlines. Orlando was just Orlando.

Thelma was different. She had a quick smile and a little giggle that, combined with her way of cocking her head at just the right angle at just the right times, made me melt into fantasies about what her touch and caress, her long legs and thin arms would feel like. But my delightful fantasies often ended in a triple-whammy guilt trip. She was a girl. She was almost normal. And she was black.

One day before English class, Thelma showed me billfold photos of her brothers and sisters, and they were also black, a fact that first startled me because I was beginning to pretend that Thelma was not all that black.

Thelma and Ann quickly became close, sharing those little secrets only adolescent girls feel important enough to whisper and giggle about in front of the boys. In some ways, I was jealous of the friendship Thelma had with Ann—the same jealousy I now felt from Ann every time Thelma would turn her attention to me. Ann knew I was infatuated with Thelma. No one had to tell her. She knew.

"Bye, Bye, Love." Strange way to put it, but it was true. I chuckled to myself, feeling delightfully free of the expectation that Ann and I were somehow made for each other and destined to be a couple. I was ready to face her disdain. I was no longer her man.

Then Russ, the boozy taxi driver who drove three other sixth graders and me to and from school, started singing one afternoon on the way home, as he often did, to the delight of his special passengers. He claimed to be a singer in one of the local bars.

"Bye, bye, love. Bye, bye happiness. Hello, loneliness. I think I'm going to die . . . ," he started crooning

"Where'd you get that?" I asked incredulously.

"A new one out," Russ, in his DJ voice, announced smoothly to his captive audience, "by the Everly Brothers—'Bye, Bye, Love'."

I sank further into the taxi's back seat—confused, hurt, and disappointed. Had I been seduced by my own wishful thinking? Maybe Ann didn't know about how I melted inside every time Thelma looked at me. Maybe I wasn't off Ann's hook, after all.

Obvious Limitations, Hidden Potential

. . . A horizon is nothing save the limit of our sight.

—Rossiter Worthington Raymond
A Commendatory Prayer

"I saw you come out of the supermarket, pushing a cart full of groceries," Mrs. Barth shouted. Her shrill voice rose above the sharp squawks of the accordion. "You put the groceries in the back seat of the car and then got in and drove away—all by yourself."

To show I was listening and understood, I nodded, surprised and amused that the incident impressed her so much that she had to describe it to me in the middle of a neighborhood wedding dance.

"I was so surprised," Mrs. Barth continued. "I didn't know you could drive."

I offered another nod. That's all I could do. The polka music bounced off the beams of the town hall as couples strutted and stomped on the hardwood floor. Any reply in my fractured speech would have gotten lost among the tuba notes, even though I was sitting next to her along a bench tucked against the wall leading to the bar.

"Jim's been driving for seven years now," my mother said during a bed of relatively smooth tuba bars. She was sitting on the other side of Mrs. Barth. "In fact, he drives fifty miles a day to and from work."

"Oh, I didn't know he had a job."

"He works at Heartland Dairies and does their newsletter," my mother offered tersely, also starting to shout above the din.

"So he drives to work everyday!" Mrs. Barth exclaimed, glancing back at me in disbelief. "Amazing . . . "

I managed a weak smile and restacked my Canadian crutches neatly underneath the bench. Yes, perhaps it was amazing, now that I began to surmise what was probably going through her mind.

Mrs. Barth's daughter, Sheri, had been my Sunday School teacher eighteen years before—when I was ten and still trying to walk without the support I found out later that crutches provided and that I needed. Every Sunday, as the Sunday School children filed into the front pews of the sanctuary, I would find myself groping for some support, and Sheri would reluctantly offer her arm to me.

I would wrap my arm through hers and walk down the aisle with her. I sought the balance she provided but, at the same time, knew I looked childish to others because I needed to walk like a five-year-old beside my teacher.

And I knew that, as a self-conscious high school student, Sheri dreaded the attention I drew to her during those few but telling seconds which punctuated my spasticity. Her brown eyes would become cold. She would stop chewing her Doublemint gum, and her lips, highlighted with passion pink lipstick, would become rigid.

I imagined the fights she perhaps had with her mother at home—all because of me. After all, what teenager would want to go through this humiliating experience Sunday after Sunday? And what mother wouldn't insist that her daughter make the best of the situation?

I could see why Mrs. Barth kept glancing at me now and then as she and my mother chatted during breaks in the music. How could a boy who could not walk unaided down the church aisle drive a car, graduate from college, or hold a job?

Sheri's pout haunted me for years, but I never saw her again after she graduated from high school. I assumed she ended up as a secretary in some office where she still chewed gum and wore passion pink lipstick. Or maybe she outgrew the gum, kept the lipstick, and became a telephone operator.

The band stopped playing, and I leaned over to Mrs. Barth, not realizing I didn't have to shout as loud or get as close to her now as I did when the tuba player was in full blast.

"Where is Sheri now?" I asked cheerfully but decidedly louder than I needed to.

"Oh, she and her husband are in Chicago. He's a dentist, and she's a psychotherapist," Mrs. Barth said with pride in her eyes. "They have two children, eight and ten."

I managed to get out the only word that came to mind. "Amazing . . . "

Stoop to Understanding

O divine Master, grant that I may not so much seek . . . to be understood as to understand . . .

—St. Francis of Assisi
Attributed prayer

The steps were broad. The railings on both sides were sturdy. I slid my hands along the railings, pulling myself up one step at a time, always putting my left foot first and then my right. Each step up in the dark took me closer to Dorene's second floor apartment. Light still streamed from the street-side window, even though it was past 1:00 A.M. and I had said goodnight to her forty-five minutes earlier.

My confrontation with Dorene was now inevitable. There was no turning back. I had driven ten miles, almost back home, then turned around in the middle of a country road to return to town during the dewy, moonlit September evening.

As I reached the top of the stairs, my chest started heaving to get more of the still night air. The landing opened into a broader space than I had first anticipated from ground level, where I left my crutches propped up against the railing at the first step.

I tried to walk straight to the door by placing my left foot and then my right in front of me, but, without my crutches, I wobbled and lost my balance. I caught the post in back of me with my left hand, regained my stability and started angrily clawing at the stoop's railing, using it for balance in a hand-over-hand series of embraces, to get to the doorway.

I had first noticed Dorene at a spring picnic for a Bible study group at my cousin's home. Although I was not part of the study group, he had invited me, and I sat on the lawn, munching potato chips and absently watching the group play volleyball in the backyard. Every time Dorene would jump to connect with the ball, she would punctuate her punch with a grunt. Her blonde hair, styled like Gloria Steinem's, would flip sensually to the left side of her face and her thick breasts would bobble beneath her blue blouse.

I was in unfamiliar and forbidden territory, for I had never climbed the stairs to Dorene's apartment before. I knocked on her door and cringed at the hollow, lonely sound. No answer. I waited, trying to put my thoughts into words that made sense. I knocked again, this time a little harder.

The porch light went on and the door finally opened halfway. Dorene peeked around the door. Her blonde, shoulder-length hair, normally flowing gently on both sides of a clearly defined part, formed a strange crisscross pattern down the middle of her head.

"Jim?!" Dorene said sternly and looked at me in amazement. "Where are your crutches?"

"Downstairs," I replied numbly. "Sorry to bother you, but I just need to ask you a question that's been on my mind a long time. How do you view our relationship?" It was the best way I could put it without degrading myself or Dorene.

"Can't we talk about this some other time?" Dorene

said coldly with a squint in her eyes. "It's late, and I'm in my nightgown."

"I know," I said firmly, "but I need you to be up front with me."

Silence.

"Come in," she finally agreed in a huff and opened the door wider.

I walked stiffly into her kitchen after placing my left hand on the door and my right hand on the doorjamb to keep my balance.

"Have a chair," she offered, uneasily. Her blue eyes, normally cold and uncaring, darted back and forth between my arms and legs in a concern I had not seen in them before.

"No, it's OK." I righted myself and stood on two legs that felt like wood. Dorene leaned against her kitchen table, her arms folded across her white, floor-length nightgown.

A daughter of a Lutheran pastor in Indiana, Dorene conducted the choirs at our local high school and at our church, where she was also a frequent soloist. She had a raspy speaking voice, which converted surprisingly into a superb soprano on Sunday mornings.

Although I did not introduce myself to Dorene at my cousin's picnic that spring, I did call her one night a couple of weeks later and asked her if she wanted to attend *The Music Man,* a production of our local theater group. To my surprise, she said yes.

Over the next six months, we would discuss a wide range of topics over quiet dinners: the subtleties of Chagall's paintings . . . the growing importance of the feminist movement . . . the theology of President Carter . . . the discrimination against singlehood. Since we were both thirty-three, being single in a coupled world and Betty Friedan's latest volley in the battle between the sexes were our favorite topics, particularly since we liked to pass haughty judgment on the current stereotypes of women at work and people with disabilities.

Educated in parochial schools and at Luther College in Decorah, Iowa, Dorene was a Lutheran feminist, which was an oxymoron in 1976. It was a confusing time for men and women. With little satisfaction, Dorene and I tried to sort out, during our dinner conversations, the differences between need and dependency, between responsibility and commitment, between empathy and love.

We had learned to share the cost of meals and tickets, although I would drive my car when we would go out together. The issue of who opened doors was no problem for us. It was whoever was the first one to get to the entrance or exit. That was usually Dorene.

Dorene would extol the virtues of her father as a rural pastor and the accomplishments of her musical family. She liked to remind me that, on any given Sunday, there were probably three members of her family (including her mother, also a choir director, and her brother, a professor of music at St. Olaf College) singing in church.

Such a religious family, I thought, would receive me as someone who was different but accomplished—someone it could learn to shower with Christian love—just as it did in adopting Dorene's younger brother.

Or would they? Dorene was quick to judge others as well as herself against her principles, which valued intelligence, knowledge, doctrine, and propriety. Maybe that was part of being a preacher's kid—growing up with the propensity to judge. Rigid judgment, in Dorene's case seemed to overshadow forgiveness, reconciliation, acceptance, and love—qualities I admired in my agnostic acquaintances as a student at the University of Wisconsin-Madison.

Dorene was intelligent and accomplished. But she was also cold—something I didn't suspect at first, watching her play volleyball in my cousin's backyard.

Was it me? Was I too much of a chauvinist to be taken seriously? Or was it my disability? Why did she seem so bored when we went out? Why did she fall asleep and sometimes snore—with her mouth open—in the front seat next to me on our trips back from concerts or plays in Madison? It was only a forty-five minute trip. I needed to find out.

Standing woodenly in Dorene's kitchen, I said again, "I just need to know where we stand, and I . . . "

"Jim . . . , " she interrupted, "I have no empathy for you—no feeling." She shook her head.

"I'm not looking for empathy," I caught myself saying, mistaking sympathy for rapport.

"I know I should, but I don't," she said quietly, ignoring my denial. She bowed her head and rubbed her brow with the palm of her right hand. "And I feel guilty about that."

"Why should you feel guilty?" I asked, sadly recognizing in her, for the first time, the agony I had felt under similar circumstances when I did not live up to the expectations of others in courtship.

She didn't answer.

"You don't have to feel guilty about this." Again I tried to assure her.

" . . . It's just that I plan never to get married," Dorene admitted flatly. Both of her open hands, small and nimble, shot out toward me. "But everybody expects . . . "

"I'm sorry," I said quietly. "I didn't understand. I didn't want to put you through this. I won't call you again."

She said nothing. I opened the door to leave.

"Can you make it down the steps OK?" she asked calmly in a false sense of concern, as if I were leaving after a casual call.

"Yes," I said firmly. Dorene had again just demonstrated why I was both attracted to her and repelled by her. Intrigued by the women's movement, she had a limited capacity for compassion, amusement, or wonder. Steeped in theology, she was not free from guilt. Freed from the church's assumptions, she was trapped by society's expectations. But I was not the right person to explore paradox with her.

She closed the door behind me but left the porch light on. I made it to the step railing unaided. In the cool, clammy night, I took a deep breath and started down the stairs, one step at a time, first the left foot and then the right, until I reached my crutches at the bottom.

As I snapped my arms into my crutches, the porch light went out.

Expectation's Edge

If we had no winter, the spring would not be so pleasant: if we did not sometimes taste of adversity, prosperity would not be so welcome.

—Anne Bradstreet
Thirty-Three Meditations

His bare chest bulged with muscles only obtained through weight lifting. His jeans gently followed the contours of his thighs. His feet tracked perfectly as he threw the football to his partner. He cringed as the overthrown ball floated beyond his partner's reach into the dorm's bushes.

He grabbed the next throw from his partner but fumbled it, ever so slightly, at the last second. Just a quick break from studying after the first week of classes, I thought.

Then I heard him cuss at the football. In anger, he heaved it to the other fellow, who dove to his right to catch it and missed it by two feet. The ball bounced haphazardly onto the ground.

I wondered how many young fellows harbor unrealistic expectations about the ease with which the basic skills of football are mastered. Perhaps the aftermath of too many Sunday afternoon football games, televised with slow motion and instant replays, I thought. Through one of the first floor rooms in the dorm facing me, I could see a black-and-white TV screen scanning the grid of a football field.

It was a warm Sunday in September, but the expectation of crisper days ahead floated through the muggy air with an occasional oak leaf, still green and succulent but tinged with blotches of yellow and brown.

Classes at the University of Wisconsin-Madison campus had just started for the 1994 fall term, and the bicycle path along the Lake Shore dorms was unusually busy. Pam and I decided to take a break from our walk and sat down to rest at a picnic table outside Ogden Hall. She was reading a book, and I was absorbing the serenity.

To be more truthful, it had been more like half a walk. Pam did the walking, and I rode beside her in my electric scooter. Now we were at our favorite stopping point, beneath the stately oaks of what was once known as the "short-course" dorms.

The cluster of oaks dotted the expansive lawn leading down to Lake Mendota's shoreline. I tried to imagine how many students, each building expectations for his or her life, had enjoyed this cathedral's shelter from summer sun and winter wind.

Three men suddenly came around the corner of the dorm, walking with purpose in a cadence that only members of the same family sometimes seem to have. The trio were grandfather, father, son, I thought, as I looked at their faces—each with a square, prominent jaw.

What kind of dreams did the grandfather and father have for the young man, who took the lead into the front door of the dorm? What pressure did he feel to trace their footsteps, to carry on a family tradition, to establish a mark of his own?

Here, thirty years ago, I wiggled my way down to the edge of Lake Mendota's water to watch the waves stroke the shore's oak roots and worn rocks and to look down into the brackish water to discover a deeper dream for my life.

At that time my dream was simple and undifferentiated: independence. A job that didn't involve physical labor. A place to live not tied to the family farm. A spouse who cared about who I was. A sense of accomplishment.

Common though they were, those dreams had propelled me through the difficult times and had come true for me. And there were extra layers of richness and heartache that I could have never anticipated as a college senior about to graduate with no prospects of a job.

A single oak leaf, one of the first to turn completely yellow and yield to its inborn fate, sliced through the still, thick air and landed on the top of our picnic table.

I wiped it off the table. It fell onto the grass, a complement to the lawn's late summer green but still out of place.

In some ways, being different had been a blessing.

When I was a year old, I had escaped death but seemed destined to live life in an institution. When I was two, my doctor said I would never walk and go to school. When I was four. I still couldn't walk.

And when I was eight, I had to take first grade over again. When I was sixteen, going to college was still an open question. When I was thirty-two, I was self-supporting but still living with my parents.

Succeeding in what others would consider basic and uneventful in their own lives had given me a sense of accomplishment others may hope for but never really achieve.

Perhaps others' expectations have fewer recognizable boundaries and, as a result, disappoint instead of satisfy when they are not fulfilled. Or maybe their dreams are redundant—a replication of what others have done—and, thus, the pursuit of those dreams fizzles into boredom.

Perhaps success and satisfaction depend upon where a person starts. As we flutter through life, we need some surprise and amazement—and the right amount of stretch.

Slim Chance

That life is worth living is the most necessary of assumptions, and, were it not assumed, the most impossible of conclusions.

—George Santayana
The Life of Reason

The aisles were narrow between rows of crystal placed with precision on fragile glass shelves. Jack walked closely behind me. His hands were ready to catch me if I fell or if my crutch accidentally brushed against a display.

I imagined shattered Waterford crystal on the floor. Just one slip or involuntary movement of one of my arms or legs would do it. It's true—I felt wobbly and tense, but I strategically placed each crutch tip in a free-fall line away from the displays as I walked carefully through the shop. The odds were with me, but to someone without a disability they probably looked slim.

"Somebody like me doesn't belong in a shop like this," I whispered to Jack. He chuckled, and I could see relief in his dancing eyes. He was thinking the same thing.

All I wanted was a Waterford goblet as a gift for Kathy, my friend and not-yet-but-hoped-for-lover back in Wisconsin. It would be a power play in our relationship—and set up the risk of rejection—but why not? When would I get back to Nassau and inside a Waterford crystal shop with prices this reasonable?

The clerk behind the counter kept shooting nervous glances in our direction as we slowly and cautiously walked through the shop.

"I'll take that one," I said without checking the price. I just wanted to get out of the shop without causing any more stress than I had already generated.

To ease the clerk's concerns, I laid my crutches down in front of the counter while I paid for the crystal by credit card. I then retrieved my "sticks" to go out the door with my package.

"I'll carry it," Jack offered.

"How am I going to get that thing home without breaking it?" I asked Jack once we were on the street.

"Don't worry about it," he assured me with a chuckle. "I'll take care of it."

It was 1981—long before relationship marketing had entered the lexicon of business, but Jack was doing it. I was one of twelve prospective buyers Jack was escorting to New Providence Island during a long June weekend in the Bahamas to look at a new condo development with units available under a time-share arrangement.

Jack had read me right. I was a high-potential prospect: a single male with a solid job who needed an escape from the pressures of work at least once a year. I was thirty-eight (about his age), had crutches, but knew how to travel.

"You're a gambler," Jack joshed later, when I bought a single bedroom, oceanside unit for the first week in February. That was a little strong, I thought. At the time I believed what he meant was that I was a risk taker. I could visualize what he must have seen in one of his sales training classes—a chart which divided prospects into categories: conservator, risk taker, entrepreneur, etc.

But he was probably right. I now had a week in the Bahamas every year with no companion. Did I really want to spend the first week in February each year on the beach alone? No. I bought the time-share week on a chance I would have a friend or a companion in the next ten months.

That convoluted rationale made sense to me then and still does today. After all, every day presents choices. It's always tempting to play it safe, stay home, and gradually mummify. Yet I force myself to go out into the world and risk rejection, ridicule, or failure that can ultimately eat away at my self-esteem because there's always an outside chance I can meet a snippet of acceptance, high regard, or success to encourage me to go even further.

Either way, I'm always surprised by what each day brings and intrigued by the roll of the dice, the game of life.

At birth, I was dealt a handful of cards that didn't add up to much at the time. My brain injury could have left me deaf, speechless, spastic beyond any control, or mentally disabled. The capabilities, both mentally and physically, I received at birth depended on what portion of my brain was damaged.

Perhaps that's why my physician suddenly left the room while he was giving me a routine physical for high school.

"I'm telling you, Mrs. Hasse," I heard him tell my mother out in the hallway. "Cerebral palsy makes me nervous."

My luck of the draw was an unusual combination of muscles that are, in some cases, too relaxed and, in other instances, too rigid; a set of motor skills that are severely affected but not too limiting; and a degree of intelligence that was not touched by my birth injury. The chances of developing a somewhat normal life were slim, possible but not probable. But that's what kept me in the game.

Yes, I guess I'm a gambler after all.

Reflections from My Mirror

Look at life in reverse to take the mystery out of those significant events that, together, have shaped who you are and have given your life meaning.

—Anonymous

The shapely hips of the naked woman first drew my attention to the print. She stood there with her backside to me, both elbows slightly bent and one heel slightly raised, looking out of an opening of two blocks thick into a nebulous space of blue and gray.

Formed of blue cubes, a tiny bust of Abe Lincoln peered through one of the blocks near the woman's left calf. In two vertical blocks next to Abe, another smaller drawing of the same woman, this time leaning to look out what appeared to be the same window, brought a blotch of white light to an otherwise dark, dreary mass of blocks which framed the print.

"I kinda like it," I said to Kathy, searching for her opinion as we stopped for the second time that evening to look at the print of Salvador Dali's *Lincoln* in the shopping mall's art gallery.

"If you say so," she replied. "I just don't get it."

We were on one of our casual, Friday-night dates with no tight timetable to allow both of us, as corporate communicators, to feel free and unwind after a week of frenzy at the office. We often just shopped. And I appreciated a good friend (and an extra pair of arms) to shop with me.

"It's Abe Lincoln," I said lamely, unashamed to state the obvious. "See, here he is." I pointed with one of my crutches to the small block containing his bluish bust.

"But why the nude?" Kathy asked.

I couldn't answer. I didn't know. But still the dark mystery of the print, so evident even under the white spotlight in the gallery's window, intrigued me. It was my type of painting—bold, complicated, and unexplainable but maybe purposeful, maybe meaningful. The confusing blocks had the potential for blending together and offering discovery to those with time and patience to discern their layers of meaning.

"Dali doesn't do it for me," she finally admitted. As a publication editor, she often lapsed into the habit of summarizing her thoughts into grabbers that would make perfect headlines, in 36-point Garamond, for two-page feature stories.

"Great alliteration," I teased. "Dali does do it . . ."

"Oh, hush," Kathy interrupted with a playful rebuke.

Standing behind the counter, the gallery's manager overheard Kathy's reply to my string of "D's" mixed with what probably sounded to her like mumbled vowels.

"Can I help you?" she called to Kathy, ignoring me.

I decided to ignore the manager, too, and said nothing.

"No, thanks," Kathy said a bit coldly, raising her left eyebrow in dismay. "We're just browsing."

We moved deeper into the gallery, pretending to browse.

"I like it," I continued. "I need something for my bedroom."

"I don't know. It's not that restful," she offered. "I'd want something more pastoral and reassuring."

"No, it'll be great," I countered with a chuckle. "Right above the headboard, so I can see it in the mirror on the opposite wall when lie in bed. I need Dali in my bedroom."

"A nude above your bed?" Kathy scoffed, lowering her voice as she glanced back at the manager, who was now at the other end of the gallery. "That's gross!"

"No, that's not the point," I cajoled. "This has meaning, depth . . . "

"You don't even know what it means," Kathy, calling my bluff, said with a smile of disbelief.

"But that's the challenge," I insisted. "I like something that can grow on me."

"A nude can grow old pretty fast, buddy—especially above your bed," Kathy joshed.

"I don't care about the nude," I mumbled, surprised we were still talking about the most obvious feature of the print.

"If you want to get it, I'll haul it to the car for you."

It was an offer I couldn't refuse. Shopping on crutches was tedious, slow, and tiring for me. But actually buying something larger than a pad of paper or heavier than a bottle of shampoo (such as a 24-by-36-inch framed print) and carrying it to the car presented one more problem—in addition to store managers who make quick judgments.

I watched the confused look on the gallery manager's face as I handed her my gold credit card. Signing the sales slip with my crutches dangling from my arms, I thanked her as I looked into her still-disbelieving eyes.

Kathy not only carried the print to the car but also carted it into my condo and hung it above my bed. In the gallery, I had tried to envision how the print's colors would complement the earth tones of my bedspread, drapes, and carpeting. They did.

And my hunch was right. After Kathy left, I plopped down on the bed, and from pillow height I could see the print's full reflection off the mirror on the opposite wall above my dresser.

Yet there was something strange about the print I still didn't understand.

Not until six months later, when I had dimmed the lights one night and sat on the foot of my bed did I see that, above the naked woman's head, was a faint line drawing of Christ on the cross. It was mixed with a splash of orange-red and was both recognizable and obscure. The print showed the crucifixion from above—a new perspective, and that's another reason why I hadn't seen it before.

The promise of freedom from bondage for us all through the crucifixion. The hope for freedom from slavery for us all through Lincoln's Emancipation Proclamation. The search for freedom for us all through the women's movement. It all came together for me in that instant.

And then I saw it—but not until I had dimmed the glaring lights, ignored the obvious, and looked at the abstract fringes of the picture in reverse through my bedroom's mirror: The rim of dark blocks which outlined the print formed a large bust of Abe Lincoln.

Beyond Success

Need and struggle are what excite and inspire us; one hour of triumph is what brings the void . . .

—William James
Life Worth Living?

The brown leather chair squeaked with every squirm I went through in trying to get comfortable for my meeting with the president.

"OK," Bob said in a deep breath as he closed the door to his office and took three wide strides to his desk. A graying man in his late fifties, he sat down across from me and paused as his eyes ran across the horizon that spanned his corner office windows.

He cupped both palms and slid them down his jaw. Bob and I had worked together for twenty years, but today was the first time I had noticed the age spots on the back of his hands.

"I've thought a lot about our conversation last week," he started slowly, "and I just wanted to check with you about whether you have any reservations about your decision."

"No," I said confidently, surprised that he expected I would have second thoughts. "This is something I've been thinking about for at least two years. I want to retire and start my own business."

"I just wanted to make sure," Bob said more abruptly, as he leaned back in his high-backed chair. Somehow he moved in his chair without causing the leather to squeak. "It's a big step."

"Well, at this stage in my life, I'm prepared—financially and emotionally—to take on some new challenges," I admitted. "It's not going to be easy, but at the same time I'm excited about it." It came out just as I had rehearsed it the night before.

"It sounds like you've really thought this through," Bob observed. I gulped because I knew the failure rate among people who try to start small businesses was about eighty percent after the first five years.

"It's called contract employment," I said with a chuckle, knowing he always became amused when I would throw around the latest buzz words from my cadre of business gurus.

"That's right. I'll have to remember that term—'contract employment'."

"Actually, I consider myself more of a counselor than a consultant—a counselor for managing change. Doesn't that sound slick?" I said lightly with another chuckle.

I knew it was going to be tough. I needed to help my potential clients look beyond my disability so they could get to know me as a person who can build collaborative, trusting relationships with them and provide them with valuable services.

"No, that sounds good," he said more earnestly. "You could be quite successful. You really have done quite well for yourself here. Married. New home."

My left foot involuntarily kicked back, hitting my

crutches on the maroon carpeting as I leaned further forward with my elbows on his desk.

True, I had achieved my dreams. I had developed a satisfying career in corporate communications. Single until I was forty, I married Pam, and we built a new home.

Beyond that, we didn't fit corporate life. We didn't have a family. We didn't have kids who played high school football or basketball. Therefore, we didn't go to Friday night games at the local high school. In fact, sports were not part of our lives. But home, family, and security—and sports—were prominent values in rural Wisconsin.

"Yeah, I basically have no debt," I said, following his lead, "so it's a good time to establish my own home-based business. That's part of the game plan."

"How old are you now?"

"Fifty-one."

"Retirement is something I'll be looking at in a few years, too," he said, reflectively. "You'll probably have a more difficult time adjusting than I will."

I didn't know what he meant. I was ready to market my skills, developed over nearly thirty years of experience in business, and I was excited about it.

Then I realized what he was saying. Establishing my own business would be more difficult for me because I could not speak clearly. I was not as mobile as others because I used crutches. Due to my physical limitations, I worked more slowly than others.

"I think we need a new definition of retirement," I finally said, trying to define how I perceived my situation. "Getting established is going to take time and a lot of hard work. But I'm trying to establish something I can do beyond sixty-five."

"You're making the right move," he said, visibly relieved that I had no reservations about leaving. "Our industry—and our company—are going to go through some tremendous changes during the next few years."

"Yes."

I had managed the company's corporate communication function for him during the last seventeen years. I had helped facilitate his strategic planning and visioning process and had helped him position the company to take advantage of merger and acquisition opportunities as the industry went through its restructuring process. The company no longer needed me.

My skills for forging links between people so that they are willing to work together effectively were needed elsewhere. Information technology, governmental deregulation, and global markets were prompting businesses to adopt a more participatory management style. And I wanted to be a part of that action.

"The more I thought about your retirement, the more it became clear to me that health insurance is going to be a key part of the package we come up with," Bob said, at last focusing on the point of our meeting. "You ready to review your proposal?"

"Sure."

How Does Savoring Satisfaction Apply to Your Situation?

1. When has a child-like simplicity helped you put life's challenges into perspective?

2. In which cases have you been surprised by your own hidden potential?

3. Under what circumstances have you made a special effort to understand someone else's perspective?

4. How have you succeeded in obtaining an out-of-reach goal through extra effort?

5. When have you taken a calculated risk and won?

6. What is helping you discover your life's purpose?

7. What inspires you to fulfill your life's purpose?

About the Author

James R. Hasse, ABC, was born with cerebral palsy in 1943. Doctors, at the time, told his parents he would never walk or go to school. But when he was seven, he did learn to walk and he did start school.

Today Jim is senior consultant for CommSciences, Inc., a strategic communication research firm based in Los Angeles. He specializes in preparation and follow-up consultation for company CEO's, corporate communication executives, and public agency administrators in the Midwest so they can make the best use of today's cutting-edge tools for communication research.

He self-syndicates a newspaper column, "When You Don't Quite Fit The Mold," about how readers can achieve freedom from false assumptions they have about themselves—and those others may tend to form about them—because they don't quite fit accepted norms. He is a charter member of The Writing Academy, founded by Dr. Harley A. Swiggum.

Jim also counsels employees about how to deal effectively with on-the-job issues that often arise because they happen to have apparent or non-apparent disabilities.

In 1965 Jim joined Wisconsin Dairies Cooperative after graduating from the University of Wisconsin-Madison's School of Journalism, where he earned a B.S. degree with honors in journalism and advertising. Jim retired from Wisconsin Dairies in 1994 after twenty-eight years of service to form his own consulting business, Hasse Communication Counseling.

During fifteen of those twenty-eight years, he reported to the president of Wisconsin Dairies—first as communication director for seven years and then as vice president-communication for eight years. Most recently he served as the company's organizational development officer and was in charge of developing the organization's strategic planning function and management system.

Jim has mentored dozens of people, some of whom are now in leadership positions for major firms.

Due to his cerebral palsy, Jim walks and talks with difficulty. Yet, in 1995 he became one of only 600 members of the International Association of Business Communicators to achieve accreditation.

In 1994 he received the Cooperative Spirit Award from the Cooperative Communicators Association (CCA), a national professional group, and the Cooperative Builder Award from the Wisconsin Federation of Cooperatives. He was the 1995 recipient of CCA's highest recognition for a corporate communicator, the H.E. Klinefelter Award.

Jim has traveled globally, including Europe, Africa, the Caribbean, and the Pacific Rim.

He lives in Baraboo, Wisconsin, with his wife, Pam.

Epilogue

As he went along, he saw a man blind from birth. His disciples asked him, “Rabbi, who sinned, this man or his parents, that he was born blind?”

“Neither this man nor his parents sinned,” said Jesus, “but this happened so that the work of God might be displayed in his life.”

—*John 9:1-3* NIV

